The Induction and Mentoring of Newly Qualified Teachers

A New Deal for Teachers

Kevan Bleach

David Fulton Publishers

London

David Fulton Publishers Ltd
Ormond House, 26–27 Boswell Street, London WC1N 3JD

First published in Great Britain by David Fulton Publishers 1999

Note: The right of Kevan Bleach to be identified as the author of this work has been asserted by him in accordance with the Copyright, Designs and Patents Act 1988.

British Library Cataloguing in Publication Data
A catalogue record for this book is available from the British Library

ISBN 1–85346–635–2

Typeset by FSH Print & Production Ltd, London
Printed by The Cromwell Press Ltd, Trowbridge, Wilts.

Contents

Acknowledgements

This practical guide to the induction and mentoring of newly qualified teachers has its origins in the Postgraduate Certificate in Mentoring course that I developed at Wolverhampton University School of Education in 1998–99. I am indebted to my colleague, Dr Bob Preston, for his valuable comments on my original course materials. I should also like to thank the teachers who worked with me on the PGC course. I remain ever appreciative of the tolerance my wife, Susan, shows for the countless hours I spend in front of my word processor.

There are various short extracts in this book from earlier works on mentoring student and newly qualified teachers. I wish to record my gratitude to their publishers for permission to use the quotations, and to make particular mention of C. Beels and D. Powell's *Mentoring with NQTs – the Practical Guide* (C.C.D.U., University of Leeds) for the rich source of ideas it provided when delivering my Postgraduate Certificate in Mentoring course.

Introduction

I wonder how many of you who are starting to read this book can think back to what was your greatest worry in your first few weeks as a new teacher? Were you concerned about your classes getting out of control? Did you fret about whether the pupils would be interested in what you wanted to teach them? Were you anticipating how you might handle any parents who turned up at school to see you? Or did you have any anxieties about fitting into your department, or the school as an institution?

Research shows that newly qualified teachers nowadays have a common fear about having to dive in at the deep end. Most schools recognise the need to overcome any sense of anxiety, numbness or isolation they experience. So efforts are made to ensure they do not feel alone in facing challenges, such as the ones above, by providing a structured programme of induction. And many schools also think it is important to allocate a mentor to new teachers to help them through their first year – especially if the going gets tough. The mentor fulfils many functions. He or she provides a sympathetic and confidential ear, is familiar with school policies and practices, and offers constructive advice. Patience and perseverance, caring and encouragement are just four of the mentor's essential traits.

I use the words 'most' and 'many' schools because for the last seven years there has been no statutory obligation for new teachers to serve a year's probation, or for schools to have structured arrangements in place for their guidance and assessment. The old probationary year was abolished by Kenneth Clarke in 1992 as part of his reforms making initial teacher training more school-based. However, the concept has been revived with the Government's introduction of an induction year for all NQTs from September 1999. All new teachers are now required to serve the year successfully before gaining fully qualified status.

When the proposals of the Department for Education and Employment (DfEE) were first mooted in May of last year, they were described in the *Times Educational Supplement* as a mix of 'pressure and support'. Focusing on both entitlements and expectations, the new induction arrangements will ensure every NQT should:

- teach only 90 per cent of the average contact time for other teachers at their school;
- have opportunities for contact with good schools and experienced teachers;
- be mentored, observed and counselled regarding their progress by their line managers;
- receive training and professional development based on an ongoing needs assessment identified via their Career Entry Profiles;
- experience provision for pupils with special educational needs (SEN);
- network with other NQTs.

At the same time, rigorous Induction Standards have been specified against which newly qualified teachers must measure up successfully. This is in addition to meeting, on an independent and prolonged basis, the existing Standards for the Award of Qualified Teacher Status (QTS). The new standards relate to familiar areas like pupil achievement, motivation and behaviour, SEN, multi-culturalism, assessment, parental liaison, use of support staff, school policies and professional development. Unless there are exceptional circumstances that merit an appeal to the Secretary of State, new teachers will be given just one crack at completing their induction year. Local education authorities (LEAs) have been allocated a quality assurance role in overseeing the new arrangements.

The DfEE's new induction arrangements are a key part of the Government's strategy for raising educational standards and performance. To be effective in their implementation, there is a strong onus on individual schools and LEAs to make certain essential provisions. These include the development and delivery of individualised programmes of induction for NQTs and well-targeted professional development and support for all teaching staff involved with NQTs, whether as classroom mentors, subject mentors or induction managers. The other vitally important factor is the school management team's commitment to the success of induction and mentoring. The ethos and culture of a school are what is ultimately crucial to the development of an effective programme.

The purpose of this book, therefore, is to assist school mentors and induction managers in primary and secondary schools in developing their professional practice when working with NQTs. It is based on open learning resources I devised for a year-long Postgraduate Certificate in Mentoring course for serving teachers at Wolverhampton University School of Education. My intention has been to draw upon research into identified good practice in the mentoring of both newly qualified and student teachers, so that the content of this book meets schools' practical and immediate needs. At the same time, I have attempted to provide a theoretical foundation, by reference to a wide range of literature on induction and mentoring, so that readers are well equipped to reflect on the wider, underlying issues. My hope is that the structured format of commentary and analysis, readings, case studies and activities for use in readers' own schools will prove to be supportive and accessible.

Young teachers have a wonderful range of opportunities open to them through which to make an impact on pupils' futures. Their effect will extend beyond what most of them will ever know. That is why the Government is perfectly right to make the influences good teachers have on peoples' lives the focus of their recent recruiting campaign in cinemas and on television. The key challenge facing those of us responsible for induction and mentoring is to translate such aspirations into reality for our colleagues who are about to embark upon their noble careers.

Kevan Bleach
June 1999

PART I

The Roles and Responsibilities of Induction and Mentoring

Chapter 1

The development of new teacher induction and mentoring

Key issues

- *What attempts have been made over the last 25 years to meet newly qualified teachers' induction and mentoring needs?*
- *What are the different ways we can define and understand mentoring?*
- *What are its historical origins and applications outside teaching?*

Arrangements for the induction and mentoring of newly qualified teachers (NQTs) have not been well developed until recently. Even within policy initiatives on teacher education, the question of induction received little mention, despite many fine words on the need to improve it. The early 1970s saw the present-day concept of mentoring first emerge. *The James Report on Teacher Education and Training* (1972) recommended school-based professional tutors who would introduce and guide both student and probationary teachers in developing their understanding of professional issues. Looking back, the Report was a significant pointer towards current initiatives in developing mentoring and linking initial teacher education with teacher induction.

Reading 1.1

[The new teacher]...needs practice under genial and expert supervision to develop...skills, to mature his style, to relate the theory he has mastered to the practice in which he is now involved...His wise seniors in his first school introduce him, by example and precept, to an understanding of professional attitudes and to an appreciation of what his particular school is, how it works, how decisions are taken, how parents are involved.

(James Committee 1972: para 3.8.)

Despite James' visionary impetus, there was very little funding to support such an innovative proposal. Implementation was left essentially to the whim of individual local education authorities (LEAs) and schools. The effects were inevitably patchy, since authorities were about to embark on local government reorganisation and secondary schools faced planning for raising the school leaving age to 16. Various initiatives to identify models of induction training and support took place through the 1970s, such as the Teacher Induction Pilot Schemes (TIPS). The energies and insights they generated kept alive the concept of induction, although in the main LEAs showed little interest in treating the development of systematic schemes as a priority.

Induction was further over-shadowed by the explosion of concerns generated by the 'Great Debate' of the late 1970s and by the retrenchment of public expenditure which led to cuts in LEA budgets. There was little more than the professional integrity of heads, teachers and advisers to sustain and encourage good practice. Thus, the question of induction remained largely untouched and unreformed in both policy and practice. The exhortation to LEAs in *Better Schools* (DES 1985) to develop teaching practices by building on initial teacher education was mostly rhetoric. By contrast, mentoring had become established in the USA, where it featured as a major part of district and state induction programmes. Its virtues were seen as creating an incentive for retaining new staff, increasing the commitment of experienced teachers and providing a school-based means of professional development.

The structural form that an effective induction process should take assumed increased significance when the statutory period of probation was abolished in 1992. For many years before, new teachers had to serve one year in a probationary status, with the onus for recognition as 'fully qualified' falling on the LEA. How far the old probationary system offered support and guidance and a foundation for future professional development, was the subject of three Her Majesty's Inspectorate (HMI) surveys, published in 1982, 1988 and 1993. A more recent survey, *The New Teacher in School*, covered 300 primary and secondary schools. Its findings included the following key points:

- the quality of induction programmes was highly variable;
- new secondary teachers were better supported than primary colleagues in developing their teaching methods and subject knowledge;
- neither secondary nor primary induction built on initial teacher training in a systematic way;
- assessment of classroom performance was largely impressionistic in primary schools;
- many LEAs were less well-placed to offer induction programmes because of changes in professional development funding;
- a high proportion of unsatisfactory teachers experienced poor induction in schools.

The comment about failing to build on initial teacher education experiences was particularly disturbing. New teachers need such provision in order to ensure the smoothest possible transition from initial teacher training (ITT) through induction to their continuing professional development. Such dichotomous oversight does nothing to counter the phenomenon of 'slippage', by which new teachers tend to discard much of what they have learned on their ITT courses and adapt to the dominant ethos and ways of working of their first school. Actively building on the strengths and insights of new teachers will dissipate any unconcealed pressure for unreflecting conformity.

Case study 1.1

Joanna seemed highly competent . . . because of her maturity and competence, and yet nevertheless could only derive personal confidence from an exemplary performance which, most significantly, would be judged by others to be so. She had positioned herself within the department in such a way as to present the 'acceptable face' of innovation . . . which would be more likely to offer protection from the critical judgement of others. She had internally adjusted to the norms . . . of those prevailing in the school and seemed extremely unlikely to become in the future a motive force for change. Joanna would undoubtedly be deemed a competent teacher . . . but her agenda for teaching was now heavily influenced by the transmission model of mathematical learning . . . and generally appeared to endorse the taken-for-granted assumptions of contemporary schooling.

(Burton and Povey 1996: 129)

Reading 1.2

He found that within six months of their first year of teaching, former ITE students had discarded much of what they had learned from their courses and adapted to the ethos and *modus operandi* of their school . . . In her review of the literature on the transition from ITE to primary schools, Sandra Acker comes to similar conclusions. New teachers in primary schools, she tells us, are often 'brought into line by the experience'; those teachers 'who persist in views incompatible with the dominant ethos of a particular school may become demoralised . . . and even leave teaching'.

(Sikes and Troyna 1991: 5)

As for LEA provision, any critical appraisal of their lack of provision must be viewed within the underlying context of sustained government efforts since the early 1980s to erode their influence generally. In a climate of devolved management in local authority schools – the grant maintained (GM) phenomenon notwithstanding – the delegation of in-service training (INSET) funds to schools and the shrinkage of inspector/adviser posts, the major responsibility for induction came to rest with schools. Whether these new centres of decision-making attracted the necessary amount of funding to facilitate induction is another matter.

Activity 1.1

In 1993 OFSTED ran two regional conferences at which heads and class teachers, among other representatives of the profession, were invited to discuss how best to respond to these findings. One of the consultation sessions invited participants to respond to the following questions:

- How can schools move to a stronger 'training' role during the induction of NQTs?
- What are the resource implications? Given current financial restraints, what can realistically be achieved?
- What part should the classroom observation of NQTs play in their induction year?
- What aspects of school life and practice should NQTs experience during induction?

What observations on current practice and suggestions for future action would you have offered the OFSTED conference?

Since the publication in 1993 of the last HMI survey, there have been several significant changes in initial teacher training and the induction of new teachers. Although the work of the Teacher Training Agency (TTA) focuses largely on ITT, it is also concerned with the continuous professional development of *all* teachers. In this respect, the Standards for the Award of Qualified Teacher Status (QTS) and the Career Entry Profile now provide both a framework and a vehicle for launching teachers' school-based professional development in their induction year of employment *and beyond.*

From September 1999, newly qualified teachers are once again expected to complete a satisfactory induction period. This involves setting their individual development needs within what the Department for Education and Employment (DfEE), in its consultation document, described as a general programme of 'structured support, experience and further on-the-job training'. A further set of Induction Standards is laid down, in addition to the Standards for the Award of QTS, against which all new teachers must be assessed. Taken together, they will form the first step in a framework of standards and qualifications opening career pathways to Advanced Skills Teacher, Subject Leader, Special Educational Needs Co-ordinator (SENCO) and the three national headship training programmes.

If schools are to be successful in helping their NQTs face with confidence the challenges and opportunities of their year, a structured induction programme will not, in itself, be sufficient. They also need to establish and maintain an ethos and culture of mentoring, whereby each new teacher is allocated a suitably trained mentor (the DfEE uses the term 'induction tutor') who will be responsible for enabling them to reflect on their professional experiences and develop their potential.

In recent years, the word 'mentor' has become part of the professional language of groups as diverse as business, nursing, the social services and, of course, education. In teaching, mentorship and mentor training and management have engaged the minds of those involved with ITT and NQTs in the following ways:

- publications and conferences have focused on mentoring;
- models from industry have been scrutinised;
- books and journals have examined the theory and practice of mentoring;
- in-service training courses have proliferated.

'Mentor' was the name of a character in Homer's epic poem, *The Odyssey*. He was entrusted with the care of Odysseus' son, Telemachus, while his father was away fighting in the Trojan Wars. This origin in Greek mythology points to a figure who is a wise and trusted adviser and friend. Mentoring in an organisational context probably started with the apprenticeship system between the sixteenth and nineteenth centuries, when master craftsmen handed down their knowledge and skills. In the professions, a higher level of understanding was nurtured. It involved transmitting values and attitudes that would enable the protégé to grasp the purposes and place of those skills.

A brief glance at some occupations outside teaching will illustrate the diverse applications of mentoring (see Table 1.1).

Table 1.1 Types of mentoring for three different occupations

Occupation	Type of mentoring
Nursing	Senior practitioners, or nurse preceptors, who support and assess young nurses during their ward experience
Business organisations	Used for the induction of new staff and to groom potential high-fliers, including encouraging women to reach positions of power
Civil service	In 1993 the former Employment Department used its Investors in People Initiative to support the role of mentoring in induction and professional development

There are many recent interpretations of the mentor's work. They cover roles such as trainer, developer, counsellor, negotiator, supervisor and assessor. A mentor should not be viewed as simply any one of these. The role can include *all* such relationships and, indeed, go beyond them. A broader concept of mentoring offers a more developmental perspective. This sees the mentor as a transitional figure who helps his/her protégé move from early to middle adulthood, often within the work setting, but also informally as a friend, neighbour or relative. It incorporates the roles of teacher, sponsor, guide and exemplar. This takes us away from views of mentoring that focus on the mentor as the main beneficiary and mover, to one that is more of a mutual relationship based on reciprocity and trust. The concept seems to be developing and changing as a consequence of growing interest in mentoring.

Reading 1.3

[Mentoring is]...a dynamic, reciprocal relationship in a work environment between an advanced career incumbent (mentor) and a beginner (protégé) aimed at promoting the career development of both.

(Healey and Welchert 1990: 17–21)

Activity 1.2

Consider whether Healey and Welchert have articulated a sufficiently wide view of mentoring. Are there any dimensions to mentorship that you feel could be added?

   The value of being mentored by somebody who has very recently held the same position, the role of assessment and the different mentoring needs of 'beginners' who take up management posts are three points to set you thinking.

Chapter 2

Models of mentoring

Key issues

- *What different models of mentoring relationship could schools adopt?*
- *What are the different roles of subject and professional mentors?*
- *What can be done to reconcile the needs of the new teacher and the school?*

Most of the research into mentoring has concentrated on its use during initial teacher training placements in schools, but it is possible to extrapolate relevant points as far as NQT induction is concerned. What has become clear is that mentoring roles and relationships are viewed in lots of different ways. This means there is no single model to which we can all subscribe. Indeed, to impose any one definition or concept on teachers – working in a variety of circumstances in their different schools – would be a mistake. Rather, it is more appropriate to think in terms of there being a number of dimensions to mentoring, each of which can be related to the skills exercised by mentors and the different levels at which mentoring takes place. Other variable factors include the school ethos, the attitude of senior management, the professional competence of mentors and the availability of resources.

To start, it is worth considering, in very general terms, what circumscribes the mentoring function. In essence, mentoring:

- exists in an organisational context;
- is an adult relationship;
- invariably involves an element of power dependency;
- is concerned with 'on the job' practice;
- is a means of promoting the new teacher's involvement in professional learning;
- emphasises progression from guided to independent practice.

Within these boundaries, it is possible to specify different models of mentoring. Tables 2.1, 2.2 and 2.3 summarise three models adapted from recent research. The summaries cover what are actually complex analyses. Nonetheless, they give a flavour of the different dimensions of mentoring. Each is probably best thought of as existing on a continuum, since the nature of the mentor-NQT relationship is likely to evolve during the induction year.

Table 2.1 Supervisory behaviours

Non-directive	Assumes new teacher can think and act largely unaided
Collaborative	Sees mentor and new teacher as equal partners
Directive-informational	Identifying problems and offering solutions
Directive-control	Prescribing action from 'expert' viewpoint

Source: Glickman 1990, cited in Vonk 1993: 37

Table 2.2 The 'novice-mentor' relationship

Laissez-faire (or 'swim-or-sink')	Very limited interaction
Collegial	Voluntary informal supervision
Formalised mentor-protégé	Contractual relationship
Mandatory competency-based	Emphasises new teacher status and requires participation in competency programme
Self-directing professional	Uses self-directing contract, but can include elements of preceding three

Source: Andrews 1986, cited in Vonk 1993: 32

Table 2.3 Levels of mentoring

Zero	Involves very general professional expertise not specifically related to needs of new teachers
Minimal	Offers practical support in areas like planning skills, classroom practice and organisation information about the school
Developed	Recognises learning process is complex and becomes involved with strategies like collaborative teaching

Source: McIntyre and Hagger 1992, cited in Williams 1993: 412–13

The next step in this survey of the roles and functions of the mentor takes us into some organising principles. Some approaches put great stress on *subject mentoring*. This type of work makes its priority the effective teaching of a subject. It was endorsed by the former Department for Education in its 1992 specification of basic competences of teaching. Subject knowledge and application was the first category. The competences were superseded in 1997 by the Teacher Training Agency's Standards for the Award of Qualified Teacher Status, and now the Induction Standards, which also place great emphasis on the acquisition of subject knowledge and understanding. Help with developing subject teaching skills is an obvious practical concern of the new teacher. The subject mentor in a secondary school is likely to be a head of department, while subject coordinators have a similar role to fulfil in the primary phase.

Other approaches stress the range of tasks and experiences facing the NQT. Only a proportion of them is germane to subject teaching. This more *general professional mentoring* role is likely to address issues of whole school concern. It is arguable whether such matters are better tackled once a degree of classroom and subject confidence has been acquired. Many NQTs initially look for support that centres on immediate, practical issues. Whole-school experiences – such as pastoral care, school management procedures or policies on equal opportunities and special needs – are more within the experience of a deputy head or senior teacher to deliver. However, the notion of mentor empowerment would appropriately lead to such issues being handled at departmental level, too.

Activity 2.1

We have seen in the above section that there are different models of mentoring, so it would be inappropriate to be over-prescriptive in identifying a mentor's tasks and responsibilities. Nevertheless, the core purpose of mentoring NQTs is to offer them professional support and development.

In the light of what you have read so far, devise an outline role description for yourself as a mentor. It should be grounded in your current expertise and role, but take into account at least some of the considerations discussed above.

A further dimension concerns the focus of mentoring activity. Again, this may be regarded as existing on a continuum. At one end of the line is *school-centred* good practice, while at the other is *individual-centred* practice which aims to help the NQT develop according to his/her strengths and needs. The school-centred approach echoes the business organisation's view of induction as a process for transforming the new employee into a full member of the organisation, via behavioural change and the transfer of loyalties and commitment. Such changes are best tackled as early as possible when the new member is more likely, for reasons of conformity and compliance, to accept the requirements of induction. To leave the process for a while risks letting the new recruit link into an alternative 'canteen' culture.

Reading 2.1

The objective of the induction programme is to win the commitment of the new recruit … This transformation of loyalties from previous organisations to the new employer is the part of induction that many organisations handle poorly … Guidelines for the manager should be to excite and to enthral. The new recruit needs data on the success of the firm, its size, its locations, its heroes.

(Hunt 1992: 217)

How could this process be mirrored in schools? Evidence suggests ITT courses have only a transitory influence on teachers' assumptions and practices. After six months or so in their first post, they tend to discard most of the perspectives and approaches that they learned from their courses. They adapt themselves to the aims and organisational model of their new schools. So school-centred mentoring involves quickly bringing new teachers into line with the prevailing culture and practices of their schools. It epitomises Becker's notion of 'situation adjustment' within stable organisations. Change is handed down from the top and new teachers are socialised into the norms and values, the strategies and procedures, of the institution in which they work.

This process can be categorised into four stages (see Table 2.4).

Table 2.4 Phases of induction

Anticipatory phase	School's expectations are set out on interview
Formal phase	After taking up post, formal signals given about required behaviour
Learning the expectations of work associates	Informal group norms of established staff absorbed as social props
Completion of entry process	Stress of joining organisation is over and a contribution is now made to its output

Source: Hunt 1992: 58–9.

However, an organisation is not only characterised by its goals, values and beliefs. There are the *people* who belong to it, too. Employers' and employees' expectations may well differ and organisations often rely on compromise characterising their relationships. How far new teachers can maintain the perspectives brought to their first jobs will depend partly on mentoring procedures that give scope for contributions reflecting the quality and strength of their emerging perspectives. Other factors include the ability of the new teacher to gain the patronage of more powerful mentors and whether the ethos is pluralistic and open to contributions from 'new blood'. An individual-centred model, therefore, will give the mentor scope to analyse the NQT's needs and the contribution he/she can make to the school, and then devise a flexible induction programme around that agenda. This philosophy of individual needs analysis is what underpins the use of the Career Entry Profile.

So, on the one hand we have the new teacher's pre-formed perspectives and individual needs, and on the other institutional constraints and expectations. Their inter-play is a crucial factor in how a school successfully constructs its own induction and mentoring model. If there is not a blending of foci between the needs of the new teacher and the needs of the school, the NQT could feel obliged to make internalised compromises with the existing culture of the school. Rejecting that course and following one's own convictions, of course, requires a high threshold of frustration in order to survive!

Activity 2.2

Who benefits from mentoring? An effective mentoring programme will have a beneficial impact, obviously, on the NQT. But what advantages does it bring to the mentor? What about the school?

Identify and list five benefits of mentoring for (i) the newly qualified teacher, (ii) the mentor, and (iii) the school as an institution.

Chapter 3

Teaching competences and teaching standards

Key issues

- *What did teaching competences comprise when introduced in 1992?*
- *What is included in the QTS and Induction Standards?*
- *What strengths and flaws are encountered in seeking to implement standards?*
- *Do lists of competences and standards provide an appropriate framework for the development of professional skills and qualities?*

We have referred already to the former DFE's basic competences of teaching. They were published in its Circular 9/92, which set out new procedures for the accreditation of initial teacher training courses for secondary schools and identified a much larger role for schools in partnership with higher education institutions (HEIs). It was followed by Circular 14/93 for primary school courses. Four broad categories of professional competence were established:

- subject knowledge and application;
- class management;
- assessment and recording of pupils' progress;
- further professional development.

The model had its origins in performance-based teacher education in the United States in the 1960s, which was influenced in turn by earlier notions of industrial and business management based on the analysis of work functions. It was thought that if the functions of an effective teacher were to be identified from research, new teachers could be trained to carry out specific behavioural tasks. This happened at a time of demands for greater accountability in the American schools system. So when the competence-based education and training movement (CBET), as it was known, claimed a connection between teacher competence and improved educational standards, it naturally stimulated a lot of interest in administrators and politicians.

Competence-based teacher education emerged on the educational agenda here at about the same time as the emphasis on training and national vocational qualifications was developing. The DFE's specification of competences, based on advice from the Council for the Accreditation of Teacher Education (CATE), was envisaged as a means of improving links between PGCE/BEd courses, the induction of NQTs and in-service training during the early years of teachers' careers. This echoed previous calls for a professional continuum from ITT and was a precursor of the Teacher Training Agency's present continuous professional development initiative.

The DFE's list of competences constituted a basic framework in which student and newly qualified teachers could apply their knowledge and understanding in effective practice. Yet some HEIs soon interpreted them via more detailed indicators. Several local education authorities – such as Surrey, Walsall and Shropshire – developed similar variations for use with NQTs. A strong concern was that there were omissions in the list. Critical self-reflection was one area strangely absent, perhaps because it was thought difficult to produce suitable indicators of performance. Paradoxically, many of the situations that form appropriate foci for reflection-in-action are the practical, problem-posing issues to do with knowing subject matter, developing teaching strategies, managing space and resources, and so on.

The *New Teacher Competency Profile*, developed jointly by Surrey County Council and Roehampton Institute, sought to address this deficiency by devising a 'menu' from which the NQT and mentor could choose areas for development to work through in depth. The intention was not just to help new teachers survive induction, but to encourage them to continue to grow professionally according to their individual needs and strengths. Although competence-based, it aimed to embody approaches to reflective practice and action research. Evaluations of the Surrey Profile found it provided:

- opportunities for self-assessment and the acceptance of critical feedback;
- good quality relationships between new teachers and mentors;
- a flexible structure for effectively supporting a wide variety of individual NQTs.

Reading 3.1

If competence, then, is concerned with minimum standards it follows that the development of competence must, logically, be only a part of a person's overall occupational or professional development... What is required for professional programmes is a model which allows for ongoing and continuing develop-ment... A combination of the generic and cognitive constructs of competence ...seems well suited to the field of teacher education in that it incorporates such examples of good practice as 'empathising accurately with the concerns of others', 'exercising power and authority in a manner consistent with organisa-tional goals and professional ethics' and 'self-monitoring one's own conduct'.

(Hyland 1993: 119–20)

This is a philosophical point that merits discussion. Is teaching an intuitive act that beggars its reduction into easily compartmentalised skills? Clearly, competence is preferable to *in*competence. Yet to be 'competent' as a teacher actually goes beyond the reduction of one's role to a narrow, skills-based approach. Guiding new entrants with lists of competences derived from an analysis of work functions is little more than initiation into a repertoire of craft skills. It holds potentially pernicious implications for their autonomy and professionalism. Without a means of encouraging the kind of holistic perspective that arises from a sense of professional enrichment and vocation, teaching can easily degenerate (in the words of Terry Hyland) into 'a mechanical task and product-oriented activity', requiring the NQT to conform to some pre-specified definition of what should be done.

It is a debate that should be set in the context of the 'vocationalisation' of education, with its assumption that *how* to, rather than *why*, should be the hall-mark of what is now called initial teacher *training*. Symptomatic of this mechanistic conception is the New Right's distrust of 'theory' and its notion that teaching is a 'practical ability', best learned by doing. This seems to dismiss the value of exposing teachers to academic knowledge and insights relating to professional practice – i.e. encouraging them to be 'reflective practitioners'. Yet the challenge facing mentors in schools is how to bridge the alleged gap between 'theory' and 'practice'. What new teachers need, surely, is to be equipped to reflect rationally on everyday educational practice so they understand what is appropriate ethically, as well as instrumentally, in situations they encounter.

Any progress in this field will need to go beyond the simple behaviourist model offered, first, by the DFE and, presently, by the Standards for the Award of Qualified Teacher Status and for Induction. Teachers embarking upon their new careers, obviously, need a planned programme of learning activities, but within a conceptual framework. They also need a process by which appropriate reflective activities may be negotiated, taking account of what the individual teacher's needs are at any particular time. One attempt to delineate the nature and range of *professional* competence in teaching was made by the Exeter University School of Education's pilot mentoring scheme, which organised teaching and management skills into viable systems of broader competence.

And yet...the hectic nature of the school day, the pressures of National Curriculum and examination teaching, and the lack of time in general have been cited by mentors and NQTs alike as militating *against* their ability to utilise professional wisdom and insight to good effect. Indeed, there is a view that the notion of the reflective practitioner is actually inappropriate for beginning teachers who are endeavouring to address the nuts and bolts of classroom practice. Clearly, there is a profound issue at stake here that calls for sensitive resolution in the provision made for NQTs.

Reading 3.2

The data suggest that what has been termed 'professional common sense knowledge' was the essence of what the students were wanting and receiving – 'recipe' knowledge which would help them at this early stage in their careers to operate effectively in the classroom. It may be that the concern with the 'reflective practitioner' which is current at the moment is inappropriate for… trying to get to grips with classroom practice.

(Booth 1993: 193)

Activity 3.1

A key challenge for any induction programme is to create structured opportunities for NQTs to reflect on their own practice and formulate perspectives on teaching and learning. Yet many of their concerns are about essentially practical matters. How can mentors strike a balance between offering what Eric Hoyle called an 'extended professional' view and strategies for coping or even survival?

The Teacher Training Agency's Standards for the Award of Qualified Teacher Status (QTS) replaced the Circular 9/92 and 14/93 competences in 1998. They apply to all students seeking QTS in order to work in maintained schools. The Standards describe specific aspects of effective performance and are meant to be more precise and explicit than the competences. Students must be assessed against, *and achieve*, all the Standards in order to complete successfully their courses. QTS, therefore, represents the first National Professional Qualification in the professional framework of standards and qualifications leading all the way through expert teachers and subject leaders to headship. Similarly, during induction NQTs must continue to meet the QTS Standards and all the new Induction Standards, which take effect from September 1999.

The QTS Standards fill ten A4 pages in what amounts to a detailed and exhaustive schedule, but they can be adequately summarised under the headings given in Table 3.1. In addition, there are specialist standards for students on courses for 3 to 8-year-olds and there is an initial teacher education prescribed curriculum for all primary English and Maths teachers.

Table 3.1 Standards for the Award of Qualified Teacher Status

---

A. KNOWLEDGE AND UNDERSTANDING

1. Secondary

i.   Know and understand concepts and skills in their specialist subject to degree level

ii.   Have detailed knowledge of NC programmes of study, level or end-of-key stage descriptions

iii.   For RE specialists, have a detailed knowledge of the Model Syllabus

iv.   Be familiar with KS4 and post-16 exam courses, including vocational ones

v.   Understand the framework and progression routes of 14–19 qualifications

vi.   Understand progression from KS2 programmes of study

vii.   Know and teach key skills required for current qualifications

viii.   Cope with pupils' subject-related questions

ix.   Know about and access inspection and research evidence

x.   Know pupils' most common misconceptions and mistakes

xi.   See how pupils' physical, intellectual, emotion and social development affects learning

xii.   Have a working knowledge of ICT up to level 8

xiii.   Be familiar with health and safety requirements

2. Primary

i.   Understand purposes, scope, structure and balance of NC; aware of breadth of content of NC

ii.   See how pupils' physical, intellectual, emotion and social development affects learning

iii.   Have detailed knowledge of NC programmes of study, level or end-of-key stage descriptions

iv.   For RE specialists, have a detailed knowledge of the Model Syllabus

v.   Cope with pupils' subject-related questions

vi.   Understand progression through KS1 and KS2 to KS3

vii.   Be aware of inspection and research evidence

viii.   Know pupils' most common mistakes

ix.   Have a knowledge of ICT

x.   Be familiar with health and safety requirements

xi.   Have a secure knowledge of content specified in ITT primary English, Maths and Science

xii.   Have a knowledge of their specialist subjects to A-level standard

xiii.   Have a knowledge of non-specialist subjects to at least level 7 of NC

Table 3.1 continued

B. PLANNING, TEACHING AND CLASS MANAGEMENT
1. Planning

i. Plan their teaching to achieve progression in pupils' learning through:
   - identifying clear teaching objectives and content;
   - setting class, group and individual tasks which challenge pupils, including homework;
   - setting appropriate and demanding expectations;
   - setting clear learning targets built on prior attainment;
   - identifying SEN pupils, the very able and those with English difficulties
ii. Provide structured lessons with pace, motivation and challenge
iii. Make effective use of assessment information
iv. Contribute to pupils' personal, spiritual, moral, social and cultural development
v. Cover exam syllabi and NC programmes of study

2. Teaching and class management

i. Ensure effective teaching of whole classes, groups and individuals
ii. Ensure sound learning and discipline
iii. Establish a purposeful working atmosphere
iv. Set high expectations for behaviour and use well-focused teaching to maintain discipline
v. Establish a safe learning environment
vi. Use teaching methods that keep all pupils engaged through:
   - stimulating intellectual curiosity and fostering pupils' enthusiasm for the subject;
   - matching approaches used to subject material and pupils;
   - structuring information well as the lesson progresses;
   - presenting key ideas, using specialist vocabulary and well-chosen examples;
   - giving clear instruction and well-paced explanation;
   - effective questioning to provide pace and direction;
   - spotting and remedying pupils' errors and misconceptions;
   - listening to, analysing and responding to pupils;
   - selecting and making good use of textbooks, ICT and other resources for learning;
   - providing opportunities to consolidate and develop pupils' knowledge;
   - improving pupils' literacy, numeracy, ICT and study skills;
   - contributing to pupils' personal, spiritual, moral, social and cultural development;
   - setting high expectations, whatever pupils' gender, cultural or linguistic backgrounds;
   - relating pupils' learning to real and work-related examples
vii. Be familiar with SEN Code of Practice;
viii. Ensure pupils gain subject knowledge, skills and understanding;
viii. Evaluate critically one's teaching

Table 3.1 continued

C.   MONITORING, ASSESSMENT, RECORDING, REPORTING AND ACCOUNTABILITY

i.   Assess achievement of learning objectives and use to improve aspects of teaching

ii.   Mark pupils' work, give constructive oral and written feedback and set targets for progress

iii. Assess and record pupil progress through observation, questioning, testing and marking to:
   - check work is understood and completed;
   - monitor strengths and weaknesses for intervention in pupils' learning;
   - inform planning;
   - check pupils make clear progress in subject knowledge, skills and understanding

iv.   Be familiar with statutory assessment and reporting, and write informative parent reports

v.   Understand demands of level or end-of-key stage descriptions and KS4 and post-16 courses

vi.   Implement assessment requirements for 14–19 courses

vii. Recognise levels of pupils' achievement and assess against attainment targets

viii. Know how assessment data can be used to set targets for pupils' achievement

ix.   Use a variety of assessments for different purposes
   Primary teachers must also demonstrate that they know and understand teaching and assessment methods specified for primary ITT English, Maths and Science

D.   OTHER PROFESSIONAL REQUIREMENTS

i.   Know duties set out in School Teachers' Pay and Conditions Act 1991

ii.   Know legal responsibilities regarding health and safety, pupil care, discrimination, child protection and pupil sanctions

iii. Build effective working relationships with staff

iv.   Set good example to pupils by presentation and conduct

v.   Be committed to maximising pupil opportunities and expectations

vi.   Take responsibility for own professional development and keep abreast of research

vii. Understand responsibility for implementing school policies, e.g. bullying

viii. Recognise need for liaison with parents, carers and welfare agencies

ix.   Be aware of role of governors

The Induction Standards (see Table 3.2) appeared in draft form in the DfEE's consultation paper about induction and were finalised in the light of comments received. They are intended to build on the QTS Standards by:

- requiring *independent* performance in selected areas where the QTS Standards assumed support from experienced staff;
- focusing on aspects of professional practice which can be developed over a longer period than is available during ITT.

Table 3.2 Induction Standards

A. PLANNING, TEACHING AND CLASS MANAGEMENT

i.   Sets clear targets for improvement of pupils' achievement, monitors pupils' progress towards those targets and uses appropriate teaching strategies in the light of this including, where appropriate, in relation to literacy, numeracy and other school targets

ii. Plans effectively to ensure pupils have the opportunity to meet their potential, notwithstanding differences of race and gender, and taking into account the needs of pupils who are underachieving, very able or not yet fluent in English, making use of relevant information and specialist help where available

iii. Secures a good standard of pupil behaviour in the classroom through establishing appropriate rules and high expectations of discipline which pupils respect, acting to pre-empt inappropriate behaviour, and dealing with inappropriate behaviour within the behaviour policy of the school

iv. Where applicable, plans effectively to meet the needs of SEN pupils and, in collaboration with the SENCO, makes an appropriate contribution to the preparation, implementation, monitoring and review of Individual Education Plans

v.   Takes account of ethnic and cultural diversity to enrich the curriculum and raise achievement

B. MONITORING, ASSESSMENT, RECORDING, REPORTING AND ACCOUNTABILITY

i.   Recognises the level that a pupil is achieving and makes accurate assessments, independently, against attainment targets, where applicable, and performance levels associated with other tests or qualifications relevant to the subject(s) or phase(s) taught

ii. Liaises effectively with pupils' parents/carers through informative oral and written reports on pupils' progress and achievements, discussing appropriate targets, and encouraging them to support their children's learning, behaviour and progress

C. OTHER PROFESSIONAL REQUIREMENTS

i.   Where applicable, deploys support staff and other adults effectively in the classroom involving them, where appropriate, in the planning and management of pupils' learning

ii. Takes responsibility for implementing school policies and practices, including those dealing with bullying and racial harassment

iii. Takes responsibility for their own professional development, setting targets for improvements, and taking action to keep up-to-date with research and developments in pedagogy and in the subject(s) they teach

---

Both sets of Standards summarised in Tables 3.1 and 3.2 represent an attempt to specify in fine detail exactly what students on ITT courses and new entrants to the profession, should be 'taught and able to use' in terms of relevant subject knowledge and classroom practice. In that sense, they remain – like the earlier competences – essentially behaviourist by virtue of reducing NQTs' learning objectives to outcomes that can be pre-specified and measured. Many teachers and heads welcome the emphasis on effective pedagogy and believe in their appropriateness as a framework for continuing professional development.

However, flaws as well as benefits can be identified as follows.

- To pass induction, new teachers must demonstrate that they meet successfully all the Standards. While we all believe in high standards, isn't this an over-estimation of what is possible during the course of their first year of professional practice?
- Should the Standards be regarded as embodying criteria on which NQTs pass or fail, like an MOT car test? Or should they lead beyond 'competence', in a technical sense, and involve gradations in performance that recognise the development of more sophisticated patterns of, and perspectives on, professional behaviour?
- What should one be looking for in order to prove that a particular Standard has been demonstrated? Their language of precision sounds appealing, but isn't the testing of human capabilities often arbitrary and approximate? So how should they be assessed and what will count as evidence? Or will schools be left to devise their own models?
- There is a diversity of conditions in one school compared with another, e.g. deprived inner city schools and foundation selective schools. How can levels of performance by beginning teachers on each of the Standards be objectively measured in order to allow for such differences?
- Will primary schools, particularly, be able to provide the level of human and physical resource needed to enable NQTs to achieve and develop all the different Standards?
- Since some secondary schools deny new teachers access to Year 9 pupils because of SATs, or to Years 11–13 because of GCSE and A-level exams, must competency in the Standards be exercised across the full age range?
- Why do the Standards not show any recognition of 'futures' aspects of teaching and learning appropriate to the twenty-first century, e.g. developing schools as 'no defects' organisations, performance-related gains-sharing, facilitating pupils' independent learning and 'virtual' schooling, working with para-professionals or the exercise of collegial responsibility within 'flatter' team organisations?

Reading 3.3

One concern is to do with the notion of competence as a working concept. Recently, a head teacher telephoned me to ask about a student teacher being considered for a post. I said the student showed every prospect of demonstrating the required competencies. 'Yes, yes,' she persisted, 'but is she any good?'

(Webb 1996: 4)

Activity 3.2

Like competences, the QTS and Induction Standards consist of discrete strands, which could make assessment fragmented and bureaucratic. To provide a more manageable structure for assessing the QTS Standards, particularly, try to group together the strands that address similar points into broader, more 'holistic' dimensions.

Chapter 4

Career Entry Profiles

Key issues

- *What are the different ways in which the Career Entry Profile is likely to benefit newly qualified teachers and mentors?*
- *What considerations should mentors keep in mind when using the Profile with NQTs?*
- *In what practical ways can the Teaching and Induction Standards be used for target setting and action planning within the framework of the Profile?*

From 1998, all newly qualified teachers have been required to have a Teacher Training Agency Career Entry Profile. It is a document providing a summary of information about strengths and areas for further professional development arising from their assessment for Qualified Teacher Status. Its purpose is to help mentors in their first schools do the following:

- deploy NQTs effectively, taking account of their strengths and development needs identified as priorities at the end of the ITT period;
- devise an induction action plan that takes into account NQTs' own targets, school targets and any locally and nationally identified priorities;
- provide focused and individualised monitoring and support during induction.

As far as NQTs themselves are concerned, the Profile aims to help them:

- target and address their development needs and build on their strengths during induction, with a view to feeding into their longer term professional development
- assume responsibility for their own professional progress by means of target-setting and review, thereby establishing a pattern of good practice that will later assist the appraisal process and their future professional development.

The origins of the Profile lie in the 1987 HMI survey of new teachers, which recommended that they should bring with them from universities and colleges a document outlining their strengths and weaknesses. Given the different routes people take into teaching, it was thought this would enable schools to respond more effectively to new teachers' individual needs. Profiling subsequently formed a key part of the competence-based local initiatives referred to in the previous chapter. When the National Foundation for Educational Research (NFER) investigated induction in the early 1990s, it recorded the advantages of such profiling as follows:

- it is a tool for encouraging personal reflection;
- it provides an agenda or backcloth for NQT-mentor discussions;
- it offers a common language and understanding;
- it encourages target-setting and monitoring.

Use of the TTA's Career Entry Profile during the induction year provides mentors with a structured approach to their work, in addition to leading on from practice during ITT. Designed as a working document, the 1999 version is divided into three sections (see Figure 4.1).

Section A is a summary of the NQT's college/university course.

▼

Section B is an agreed statement of strengths and priorities based on performance during that course.

▼

Section C is the key developmental section where the NQT and mentor jointly engage in regular target setting and action planning during the induction year, based on the content of Section B and the particular demands of the NQT's new post.

Figure 4.1 Sections of the Career Entry Profile

The process linked to Section C in Figure 4.1 should involve treating the QTS and Induction Standards as a 'menu' from which topics can be chosen in order to prioritise and respond to NQTs' individual needs. The aim for the mentor must be to help enable the new teacher to make progress in developing his/her professional competence, always bearing in mind that this should be regarded as a continuum. One weakness in the TTA's Standards framework is the way it implies success occurs on a 'once and for all' basis in securing qualified teacher status at the end of ITT and induction. Such an approach fails to acknowledge that teaching standards can always be developed further in more challenging contexts or more complex ways *at any point* in one's career.

Selecting a few areas of focus from the Standards will allow them to be explored in depth, although in practice this is likely to involve others because of the common ground that a number share. For example, establishing a purposeful working atmosphere (teaching and class management) cannot be considered in isolation from setting challenging tasks (planning) or being able to cope with pupils' subject-related questions (knowledge and understanding).

The Profile makes it clear that both strengths and areas for concern should be explored. For NQTs, taking an area of strength or enthusiasm will be useful in developing confidence and maintaining professional interest. With an area of difficulty, there is advantage in mentors employing a problem-solving approach, whereby new teachers are encouraged to contribute their own answers to an analysis of the situation. At times, this would require mentors holding back on advice and demonstrating their ability to listen, thereby avoiding quick-answer coping strategies. Another need is for the NQT and mentor to negotiate criteria for the Standards which are 'customised' to their particular school context. Also, they are better approached developmentally, rather than judgementally. Used in these ways, the Standards and the Profile should provide a flexible means of giving individual NQTs support during induction and responding to their development and training needs. Figure 4.2 is a suggested process to follow when using the Standards during induction.

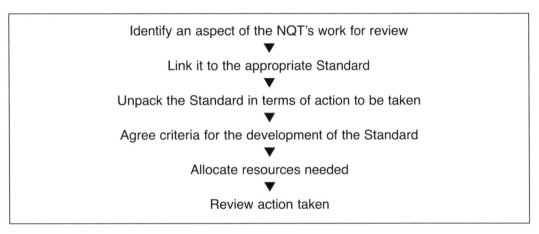

Figure 4.2 Process to follow when using the standards during induction

Ways in which critical self-reflection can be encouraged as part of the process of analysis and self-review are explored in Chapters 10 and 11. Table 4.1 (a), (b), (c) and (d) illustrates how the QTS Standards may be unpacked to facilitate setting targets with NQTs during their induction year.

Table 4.1 How QTS Standards may be unpacked to facilitate setting targets with NQTs during their induction year

(a) Knowledge and understanding			
Teaching standard	Action to be taken	Success criteria	Resources
Detailed knowledge of NC programmes of study and level descriptions.	Relate statutory guidance to a module in dept scheme of work. Produce assessment mark scheme using levels. Put levels criteria into 'pupil-speak'.	Lesson plans take account of NC programme of study. Marking of pupils' work and teacher comments expressed in levels.	Time to work with subject mentor in relating module to NC PoS. Purchase teaching support materials tied into level descriptions.
Familiarity with vocational exam courses.	Visit another school offering GNVQ in subject area to gather information on subject delivery and forms of assessment employed.	Contributes to school's GNVQ programme. Lesson observation focuses on teaching process and/or forms of evidence used for assessment.	Day visit, followed by review of findings with subject head and/or vocational studies head.
Know about and can access inspection and research evidence.	Access OFSTED inspection reports on Internet. Join professional association for subject (e.g. Historical Association) and read journals. Study GCSE/A-level examiners' reports.	Awareness of recognised good practice in subject teaching. Keeps up-to-date with latest developments in subject. Advises pupils of good practice for exam questions.	School subscribes to Internet. Membership subscription for dept staff. School library subscribes to journals. INSET on exam syllabus.
Working knowledge of ICT.	ICT coordinator to run INSET session or work on consultancy basis in classroom. Observe good ICT practice in another department.	Ability to use appropriate hardware. Aware of software suitable for classroom use. Lesson plans show evidence of ICT, e.g. use of CD-ROM.	Time for INSET or use of coordinator in classroom. Purchase of software by department.
(b) Planning, teaching and class management			
Identify clear teaching objectives and content.	Develop understanding of criteria for effective lesson planning. Understand variety of learning styles pupils use. Develop methods to assess pupils' success in meeting objectives.	Lesson plans define goals and demonstrate pace and progression. Teaching objectives are shared with pupils. Clear links between goals and teaching/ learning activities.	INSET on effective teaching and learning. Lesson observation and feedback by subject mentor.

Table 4.1 continued

Teaching standard	Action to be taken	Success criteria	Resources
Identify very able pupils.	Recognise generic and subject characteristics of able pupils. Awareness of suitable teaching methods, organisational strategies and curriculum provision.	Uses assessment data to identify able pupils in teaching sets. Focus on differentiated provision in lesson observations.	INSET on appropriate teaching, assessment and classroom management strategies. Lesson observation and feedback.
Set high expectations for behaviour and use well-focused teaching in order to maintain discipline.	Awareness of school policy and dept procedures on behaviour. Observe good practice in school. Devise ground rules for classroom control.	Has ground rules for pupil conduct. Praises and encourages. Improved pupil–teacher relations. Demonstrates efficient planning and organisation.	INSET on positive behaviour management. Observation of more experienced colleagues who successfully promote positive behaviour.
Contribute to pupils' personal, spiritual, moral, social and cultural development.	Development of form tutor's role. Knowledge of pupils' variety of backgrounds. Familiarity with equal opportunities issues. Urge to view school as moral community.	Effectively fulfils form tutor's role. Demonstrates awareness of, and respect for, pupils as individuals. Lessons reflect equal opportunities issues. Extra-curricular activities.	Meetings with PSE and Equal Opportunities Coordinators. Opportunity to explore links with external agencies and stakeholders.
(c) Monitoring, assessment, recording and reporting			
Assess and record pupil progress through observation, questioning, testing and marking.	Provide a critical awareness of the wide range of formative and summative assessment techniques available. Identify and observe examples of good assessment and recording practice in school.	Lesson plans and observations show variety of formative and participatory assessments. Pupils' work shows regular marking and constructive comments. Keeps up-to-date records in line with departmental and school policy.	INSET with Assessment Coordinator on formative and summative assessment. Time for observation of good practice in different areas of school.
Familiar with statutory assessment and reporting, and writes informative parent reports.	Knowledge of current statutory requirements. Knowledge of school procedures for reporting.	Produces detailed and well presented school reports. Reports set targets for pupils and identify ways to plan action for improvement. Reports enlist parental support.	INSET involving critically reviewing examples of reports, practising report writing and dealing with parents at consultation evenings.

Table 4.1 continued

Teaching standard	Action to be taken	Success criteria	Resources
Recognises levels of pupils' achievement and assesses against attainment targets.	Develop awareness of what constitutes achievement at different levels of attainment or in end of key stage statements. Appreciates value and limitations of NC assessment tools.	Makes realistic assessments of pupils' progress in line with level or end-of-KS criteria. Translates levels/ descriptions into 'pupil-speak' to facilitate understanding. Uses assessment data as part of planning process for individuals.	Involvement in compiling departmental portfolios of exemplary work for assessing NC levels.
(d) Other professional requirements			
Knows legal responsibilities about health and safety, pupil care, discrimination, child protection and sanctions.	Knowledge of appropriate legislation. Knowledge of school procedures for addressing legal responsibilities.	Demonstrates working knowledge of legal responsibilities and school procedures as classroom teacher and form tutor.	School handbook and policies. INSET on relevant topics, e.g. child protection, involving case studies.
Builds effective working relationships with staff.	Provide opportunities in meetings for expressing NQT views. Use NQT's strengths and interests to identify areas for contributing to school development.	Contributes effectively in departmental and pastoral team meetings. Takes part in project working parties.	Resources to support initiatives in which NQT is involved.
Takes responsibility for own professional development and keeps abreast of research.	Awareness of preferred career direction. Knowledge of suitable INSET to develop competence. Access to books and journals.	Commitment to developing professional competence. Ability to engage in professional debate on topical issues.	Meetings with senior mentor. Funding for INSET courses. Provision of educational journals and books in staff library.

Activity 4.1

Having studied these examples of how Standards can be used for target setting and action planning, take one of the Induction Standards and devise a similar schedule for an NQT in your school or department.

Chapter 5

From novice teacher to reflective practitioner

Key issues

- *What are the different stages of development that newly qualified teachers go through during their induction year?*
- *What implications does this have for a developmental approach to mentoring?*

Chapter 1 referred to Mentor, a character in Homer's *The Odyssey*. He was entrusted with the care and well-being of Telemachus, the son of Odysseus. The relationship required of Mentor was one of wisdom, integrity and personal investment. These are also key features in an effective relationship between a mentor and a newly qualified teacher. There are other traits indispensable to the operation of the mentoring role, such as friendship, understanding, sympathy, honesty and mutual respect.

In view of this, what is at stake in the mentoring relationship is the kind of person the mentor is – and how that person brings his/her whole being to bear on the fulfilment of that role, above and beyond the inculcation of classroom skills and competences. When teaching children, the good classroom practitioner does not confine him/herself to knowledge and skills and concepts. Teachers convey to their pupils not just explicit knowledge, but also their attitudes and positions, and the personal ramifications and implications that knowledge holds for them. This applies to the experience of teaching at whatever level, including the mentor's relationship with the NQT.

Further, mentoring should not be regarded as a one-way process. It involves more than the 'expert' practitioner simply guiding the 'inexpert' novice. There must be a dimension of mutuality to mentoring. This has been characterised in a number of ways, such as shared power, the mutual exchange of information, equally active roles, collaborative learning and reciprocal reflection.

Reading 5.1

The mentor must stand in the same relationship to the trainee as the trainee does to his or her pupils: as someone bringing their whole being as a person to bear rather than exercising certain skills. This, essentially, is what makes the business of learning to teach different from learning to be a gardener or a carpenter or a welder, and what makes the metaphor of apprenticeship so completely inappropriate...

(Smith and Alred 1994:106)

The framework of the mentoring relationship should advance and grow over the induction year. It should parallel the different stages of development through which the NQT goes in beginning his/her teaching career. During this time, the mentor should come to see the new teacher increasingly as a professional working colleague. The reciprocal atmosphere of their relationship – and its increasingly open, honest and relaxed nature – should develop by virtue of the more active role the NQT is allowed to play in his/her own development. Effective mentoring, therefore, may be said to involve an increasingly voluntary and equal partnership in pursuit of a common interest or shared concern.

The balance is a delicate and changing one, particularly with regard to NQTs' professional competence and insight. Initially, they are dependent on their mentors for help with subject knowledge and application, orientation to school settings, organisational arrangements and support with resources. Much of what NQTs want to learn consists of competences relating to classroom survival. They seek quick and effective access to 'recipe' knowledge, i.e. rules and routines and ways of securing greater control over their teaching and learning. This is because they often see themselves as 'double strangers', to both their pupils and other teachers. Until such utilitarian functions have been completed, there is little alternative for mentors but to act in a largely supervisory and training role. It is a time that calls for intensive support. Mentors need to help novice teachers begin to act like experienced teachers and deploy ready-made strategies for subject delivery and classroom control.

However, as NQTs begin to cope with the teaching situation and achieve some success, they will be entering the stage of confident classroom management. This is when there should grow an awareness of how children learn and teachers teach. Implicit in it is the development of their understandings and beliefs. The challenge for mentors is to create opportunities for NQTs to begin to develop their own teaching style and *persona*. In doing this, the latter will learn not just to act, but to think, professionally so that they become increasingly self-managing in terms of task and process.

Case study 5.1

Research carried out with a group of new teachers illustrated this developmental aspect of NQTs' thinking and learning. What preoccupied them at first were issues of technical competence, such as basic classroom skills. The aims and values which guided their actions seemed to be largely taken for granted. However, as the year progressed, they were searching more and more for indications of the success or otherwise of their teaching in terms of pupils' learning achievements. They reflected, as well, on just what those achievements should be. Basic teaching issues were relegated in importance, partly through routinisation, as they wrestled more and more with problem-awareness and self-evaluation.

(Abridged from Tickle 1999: 79–92)

Probably the most structured model for this continuum is the description of teacher progress identified by John Maynard and Trisha Furlong. It can be applied to initial teacher education, the first year of teaching and to further professional development as shown in Figure 5.1.

Early idealism and identification with pupils.

Survival strategy based on quick fixes
and tips for teachers.

Recognises difficulties and their causes.
Appreciates limits of what teachers can do.

Reaches a plateau, in that the teacher does not
want to upset routines that are bringing success.

Moves on to a recognition of the need to pay
more attention to the quality of
teaching and learning.

(Maynard and Furlong 1993: 69–85).

Figure 5.1 Maynard and Furlong's model of teacher progress

A broadly similar model, comprising four levels of competence, was devised by Stronach *et al.* (see Figure 5.2).

Idealised competences, in which the values and ideals
of the training course are inculcated.

Coping competences, which are developed as new teachers
learn to fit in, deal with confrontations and negotiate
an identity with pupils and other teachers.

Vernacular competences, acquired mainly through trial
and error, assisted by the advice of other teachers.

Realised competences, involving more stable relationships
with classes and the emergence of a set of beliefs
about the nature of teaching.

(Stronach et al. 1996: 81)

Figure 5.2 Stronach et al.'s model of teacher progress

Ideally, the transition from one phase of the mentoring relationship should lead into the other, although in reality it is not guaranteed to be easy. It would be better to think of it as a cumulative process rather than movement from one discrete phase to another. For some NQTs the learning curve extends naturally upwards. Others might be unwilling to move forward from seeing teaching as merely the transmission of knowledge and information. They may be reluctant to experiment with different forms of classroom organisation or grant pupils a more active role in their learning. Nevertheless, learning how to stand back from their performance and evaluate their professional practice is an essential step that new teachers have to undertake. It must also be a key priority for mentors if NQTs are to make the necessary transition.

Encouraging new teachers to develop reflective qualities is an area of professional development for mentors significantly lacking at the moment. Problems can arise because of unfamiliarity with this aspect of the role, misperceptions of what it entails, or unease about relinquishing a superordinate function. In primary schools, lack of non-contact time is a problem in enabling mentors to develop their role beyond mere supervision. Realistically, there will still be times when it is appropriate for mentors to remain assertive in the influence they exert. If there is a danger that the new teacher is 'drifting', he/she will need continued steering in an appropriate direction.

Despite this, the kind of assistance ultimately beneficial to NQTs is that which can be offered by an experienced but, in certain crucial respects, equal working colleague – a professional partner who encourages them to reflect actively and self-critically in order to develop their perspectives on teaching and learning. It is here that McIntyre and Hagger's concept of developed mentoring (referred to in Chapter Two) becomes relevant, with its emphasis on collaborative teaching and planning.

Reading 5.2

Until learner-teachers have demonstrated that they have developed the competence necessary for them to be deemed suitable entrants to the teaching profession, there is no way of escaping the need for mentors to be authority figures who, in teaching and assessing, may have to make unilateral judgements about what is satisfactory and what is needed . . . [Later on] it is the learner-teacher who should be now taking the lead in setting agendas; and while his or her 'partner' may have more knowledge or information of various kinds to contribute, the judgements of the learner-teacher are now recognised as the important ones.

(McIntyre and Hagger 1994: 100)

Activity 5.1

Discuss with an NQT in your department or school what his/her needs for professional development were at the start of the year. How have they changed or developed as the year has progressed?

In this new supervisory partnership, mentor and mentee can learn to understand and accommodate – and sometimes to challenge – each other. The mentor must enjoy being involved in learning because this continuous engagement with someone else's development will inevitably contribute to his/hers. Crucial to this transition is the degree of personal and professional strength, the sensitivity and the insight characterising the mentor–mentee relationship. It holds interesting implications for the integration of mentoring and appraisal as a long-term aim.

It is possible, also, to interpret a merging equivalence between mentors and NQTs in postmodern terms. A core theme of many postmodern thinkers is the 'implosion of boundaries'. The age of modernity was characterised by an active superiority that designed ways of life into which others had to fit. However, such assumptions are now less acceptable in view of the scepticism with which previous certainties are regarded. There is also the influence of discourses from the business world. Schools cannot be impervious to such changes. That is why, in education, management and leadership are the subject of critique and redefinition, leading to a trend away from traditional hierarchical control mechanisms. The notion that all groups should be free to speak for themselves applies perfectly reasonably to the mentor–NQT relationship.

Part II

Developing Relationships in Induction and Mentoring

Chapter 6

The qualities of effective mentoring

Key issues

- *What factors does the success of the mentoring relationship depend upon?*
- *Do the qualities needed to be a good mentor vary between primary and secondary schools?*
- *Is there a necessary tension between the counselling and assessment roles of mentorship?*
- *What implications are there for mentor selection, training and resourcing?*

Researchers in Britain and elsewhere have identified a wide range of qualities needed for effective and successful mentoring. Essential prerequisites include the ability:

- to encourage, empathise, listen, reflect, analyse, organise, be flexible and be approachable;
- to establish a supportive supervisory relationship, apply effective counselling skills, and support the development of effective classroom practice.

Mentors should be people-oriented, value their work and *like* their less experienced colleagues. They need to be nurturing, insightful, protective and knowledgeable. The supportive mentor is a good role model with a sound subject knowledge, challenging teaching style, sympathetic but firm manner, high standards, loyalty, commitment in time and effort, and good communication and counselling skills. A strong factor in the selection of mentors, therefore, should be their credibility as practitioners – although it is not necessarily productive for them to be seen as role models if new teachers are to be encouraged to develop their own professional practice.

A clear emphasis on the *importance of interpersonal skills* and relationships emerges from all these characteristics. It is not difficult to guess why. The basis of the relationship is the new teachers' need for assistance. In many ways, they are strangers seeking access to a new society – the classroom as the particular place of work and the school as the work organisation. Their first year is often characterised by a burden of frustration, anxiety and doubt about their sense of self and the tasks confronting them. Consequently, the mentor is looked to with anticipation. He/she is the person who will provide a quick and effective induction to the new school environment, thereby helping their emotional survival and ensuring that the experience does not become a painful rite of passage. In this respect, it can be beneficial for NQTs to have a 'buddy'-type mentor who is recently qualified and thus well-placed to understand queries and concerns that might not appear so pressing to more experienced staff.

Reading 6.1

Supportive Mentoring

Good role model with good knowledge of subject, challenging teaching style, good pupil and staff relationships, sympathetic but firm manner, insistence on standards, follows procedures and shows loyalty to others, commitment in time and effort, enjoyment of communication, counselling and monitoring activity, sees the student as a personal responsibility.

Adverse Mentoring

Poor role model with limited knowledge of subject, pedestrian teaching style, abrasive pupil and staff relationships, withdrawn or cynical, sloppy in procedures, ready to blame others, has little time for [NQT], sees the work as a chore, little contact with [NQT] except when required by crisis or formal procedures.

(Glover *et al.* 1994: 27)

Research suggests that the quality of the *protégé–mentor relationship* is one that can make or break new teachers. Where problems are encountered or a low level of success is achieved, the new teacher often has had ineffective support from – or an unproductive relationship with – their mentors. A two-year research project on the management of induction in five LEAs showed that, at the opposite extreme, all the new teachers who made high achievements received a strong level of support from mentors with whom they enjoyed good relationships.

These relationships were based on the mentor doing the following:

- maintaining frequent contact;
- allowing observation of his/her own lessons;
- engaging in detailed feedback discussions;
- praising achievements;
- suggesting new approaches.

Case study 6.1

Two new infant teachers who worked in open plan schools and shared a teaching space with their designated teachers spoke highly of the situation which enabled observation, feedback and even active training to be carried out in an unthreatening everyday context. In a country junior school another two young women were mentored by the deputy head who made a point of seeing them every day... allowing them to observe her, working jointly with them and having regular detailed feedback discussions... She monitored their planning and evaluations and praised their every achievement, whilst suggesting new methods and approaches to extend their skills.

(Turner 1999: 33)

Where this strong relationship occurs – with the new teacher being assisted in ordering, structuring and reflecting on experiences – the mentor may well find him/herself functioning as a role model. Conversely, the self-confident and knowledgeable new teacher would clearly find it uncomfortable trying to relate to a mentor for whom listening with empathy, or offering advice rather than dogma, did not come easily.

Successful mentoring, therefore, possesses a strong *personal* as well as professional aspect. It involves one in the new teacher's professional growth and it involves one with him/her as a human being. A mentor must have 'two sides': a personal, befriending side and a professional side. A mentoring relationship that is formal in structural terms does not have to be formal on a personal level, although the ethos of the individual school may well affect the extent to which this becomes possible. This has implications for both mentor selection and mentor training.

Reading 6.2

NQTs are having to manage a lot of change at one go – they've got the demands of their first job – with all that entails – at the same time as they are coping with moving to a new area, finding a place to live, settling in and so on. Put all that together and it's obvious that sometimes things get difficult and they can need help.

(A primary head teacher, quoted in Beels and Powell 1994: 15)

This brings one firmly into the affective dimension of learning for new teachers, which is significantly lacking in both the QTS and Induction Standards. Just as it is widely accepted that children learn best if they are happy, so the personal dimension of learning is a crucial aspect of new teachers' induction. Many have told researchers that the most satisfying aspect of being mentored has been the relationships established. They have also reported that the help they value most from mentors is personal in nature, i.e. general support, encouragement and discussion.

The role of the affective dimension in mentoring is very important. The implications carried with it could be explored in considerable depth. Suffice it here to state that the 'constructivist' view – that learning for children and adults involves the construction of knowledge through first-hand experience – includes emotion as an integral part of this learning. Feelings such as frustration, anxiety and disappointment are both inevitable and valuable aspects of learning, although they exist on a knife-edge between a challenge that can be resolved and a threat that cannot.

For professional growth to occur, new teachers need to face challenges to their previous ideas about teaching and learning. However, accompanying this must be a mentoring relationship that provides a high level of support and bolsters their feelings of self-confidence and self-esteem. It should reflect the fact that one is working with, and understanding the needs of, *adult learners*. This offers the potential for professional learning via a social process, to which talk is central, where social interaction is encouraged and cooperatively achieved success is the major aim. Mentoring, therefore, becomes a two-way process, by which the participants recognise that they can learn through each other within the context of a relationship that develops through time in a collaborative learning environment.

Reading 6.3

Professional learning within the context of a mentoring relationship, conceptualised as being developmentally beneficial to both mentor and mentee, has a number of key factors. In the first place...the participants are learning *through* each other in a collaborative manner. Secondly, the learning takes place in the context of a relationship which changes over time. Healy and Welchert (1990) suggest there is a developmental sequence in the relationship which is affected by a number of factors...They describe an initial stage in the relationship when participants get to know each other...followed by an intense period of cultivation (or development) which is when most learning occurs. This then wanes as mentor and mentee distance themselves and separate. At this juncture they either redefine their relationship in a collegial way or suffer a deteriorating alliance.

(Boydell 1994: 40–41)

Elliott and Calderhead have also explored affective aspects of the professional growth of new teachers. They recognise the importance of challenging their pre-existing ideas, but emphasise the process must be done supportively if the greatest growth is to occur (see Figure 6.1).

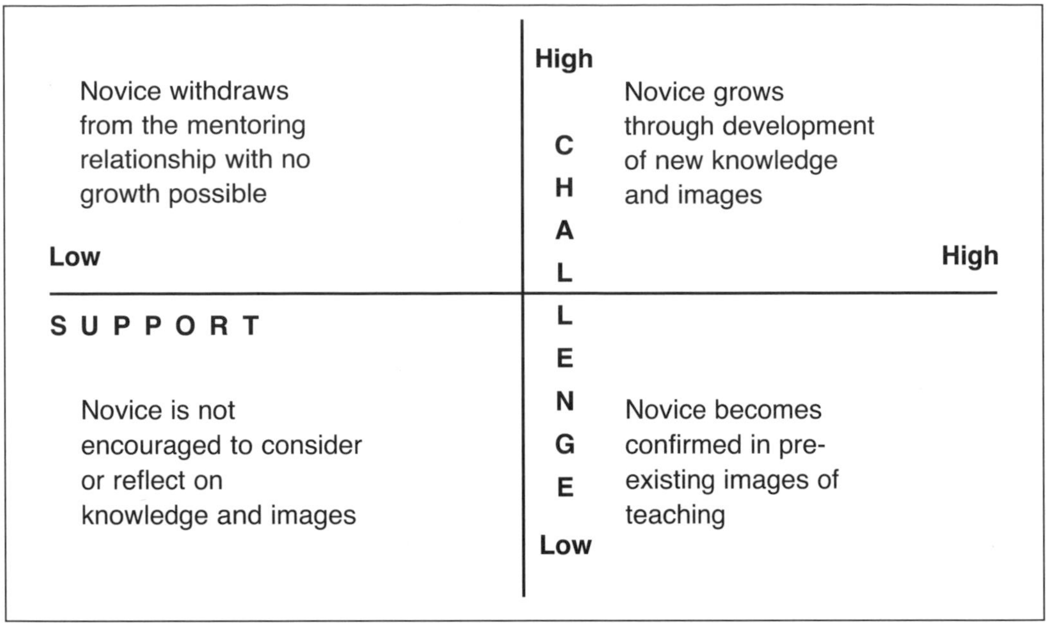

	High	
Novice withdraws from the mentoring relationship with no growth possible	**C H A**	Novice grows through development of new knowledge and images
Low	**L**	**High**
S U P P O R T	**L E**	
Novice is not encouraged to consider or reflect on knowledge and images	**N G E**	Novice becomes confirmed in pre-existing images of teaching
	Low	

(Elliott and Calderhead 1994: 172)

Figure 6.1 Two-dimensional model of mentoring relationships

The distinguishing characteristics of an appropriately high level of support include:

- fostering the professional development of new teachers;
- a socially interactive and evolving mentoring relationship;
- an emphasis on cooperatively achieved success;
- opportunities for reflection as part of the NQT's learning process;
- professional development for mentors to enable them to help NQTs be positive about the role of their feelings in learning.

It is interesting to note the differences of emphasis between primary and secondary schools regarding mentoring qualities. In the NFER's survey of induction in 30 schools and six LEAs, NQTs and mentors identified the key skills and qualities they looked for in a mentoring relationship. Tables 6.1 and 6.2 summarise their responses in rank order.

Table 6.1 Mentoring qualities valued by NQTs

Secondary NQTs	Primary NQTs
•supportive/shows genuine interest/ always asks how I am doing •a good listener •honest/open •well-organised/efficient •non-judgemental/neutral •gives ideas/shares resources •offers reassurance •available •someone you can trust/feel comfortable with •communicates skilfully •accessible •gives practical advice/guidance	• prepared to give quality time/willing to find time for you • a good listener • approachable • someone to respect/look up to/good at job • someone you can trust/feel comfortable with • empathises with newness/puts themselves in your place • a friend • honest/open • non-dogmatic/doesn't impose their views • gives ideas and resources • accessible • gives practical advice/guidance

Table 6.2 Mentoring qualities that mentors believe NQTs value

Secondary NQTs	Primary NQTs
•experience/skills/strategies •readiness to listen •approachability •giving practical advice •anticipating problems •responsiveness/flexibility	• approachability • readiness to listen • supportiveness/'just being there' • experience/skills/strategies • giving practical advice • someone to confide in/honour confidentiality

(Earley and Kinder 1994: 78–9)

Activity 6.1

Note carefully the differences of emphasis between the responses from the primary and secondary schools.

Primary responses emphasised 'giving time' as the key issue and also stressed the value of affective qualities and the notion of 'equivalence' in relationships (i.e. friendliness, empathy, approachability). What do these nuances suggest to you?

Secondary NQTs mentioned 'neutrality', good organisation and communication skills. What do these responses imply regarding NQTs' appreciation of the role of the mentor?

So far, so good on the qualities that should characterise the mentoring relationship. Now for a thornier issue: to what extent should the mentoring function include *assessment* of an NQT's performance?

This tends to be a disputed area. The mentor is the obvious person to fulfil an assessor's role. Yet there are potential problems in sustaining a relationship that involves supporting and challenging and, ultimately, assessing an NQT's teaching competence. Experience on the Articled Teacher Scheme showed that the temptation was to take the easy option and line of least resistance and say that a new teacher had 'passed'. It is a particularly delicate issue if questioning an NQT's competence leads the *mentor* to feel he/she has failed. Or there may be an implication that the school is deficient in terms of providing a supportive environment.

It is understandable that mentors feel susceptible to pressure to be reassuring rather than challenging, however important they recognise the issue of quality assurance to be. Holding the lever of assessment does involve a formal balance of power that is unequal and that could be construed as inimical to the kind of ideal mentoring relationship signposted in this section.

Some researchers believe the tension can be avoided by making a clear distinction between the two sides of mentoring. The mentor should be a person assigned specifically to guiding the novice teacher, while somebody else acting in a supervisory capacity should exercise the assessment role. However, this ethical dilemma is surely not insurmountable. What partly holds the key to *combining* the guidance and assessment roles is the quality of the professional relationship between the mentor and the NQT, and the extent to which the latter is accorded a shared ownership of the assessment dimension.

Reading 6.4

In recent literature, the terms supervisor and mentor are used simultaneously which often leads to confusion. However, we propose to make a clear distinction between the two. A mentor is a person assigned only to guide the novice; a supervisor combines guidance and assessment. In the case of a mentor, teacher assessment can be done by others, e.g. school management... Our research and training practice leads to the conclusion that, if a clear distinction is made between guidance and assessment, assigned well-trained mentors can play a crucial role in the induction process of beginning teachers.

(Vonk 1993: 32–3)

If schools are to witness the development of quality mentoring relationships that combine the roles of guidance *and* assessment, two crucial issues must be faced:

• how mentors are selected;
• the subsequent development and resourcing with which they are provided.

Both are essential inputs if the manner, quality and frequency of mentors' support for their new teachers is to be successful. Research in the late 1980s found that teachers' comments on the teaching of others could be subjective and judgemental, rather than objective and analytical. It is an encouraging sign that the advent of mentor training by universities, in-service courses addressing appraisal and the introduction of departmental self-reviews have all contributed to provide many teachers with greater skills in the observation and analysis of classroom teaching.

If, however, the role of the mentor as what Eric Hoyle called an 'extended professional' is to be developed, the process of mentor education must gain momentum. The fact that a few universities, such as Warwick and Wolverhampton, are starting to offer courses for mentors is one very helpful contribution. Schools themselves must play their part in terms of deliberately nurturing a mentoring environment. If the culture and ethos of a school, for instance, does not lend itself easily to teachers sharing problems, both new and experienced staff will have reservations about being candid with each other. The model of teaching should convey an impression, not of isolated activity, but of collective support and problem-solving.

To hark back to the Greek legend of Mentor, the practice of the Greek warrior class was to assemble as peers so that issues could be placed in the public domain and treated as matters of common concern. Warriors' relationships with each other were defined in terms of equality, rather than superordination and subordination. It is from such a cultural setting that inspiration should be drawn in taking steps to create an active mentoring climate firmly rooted in reflective practice.

Head teachers who are committed to mentoring should designate as mentors teachers who are reflective professionals – practitioners who go beyond the assessment of classroom skills to examine the theoretical dimension and questions of values. They should give them an adequate time allocation and realistic role definition to assist them in working with NQTs. The general benefits would become evident in areas like the improved performance of new teachers, mentors and pupils through increased concentration on classroom practice, improved management skills, and counselling, negotiation and the setting of targets.

Reference to 'Greek warriors', of course, unwittingly points to another dilemma, viz. the extent to which there are differing needs and wants in mentoring relating to gender.

Some researchers argue there is no innate difference in functioning between male and female, while others point to different ways of perceiving work. For instance, in a male mentor/female mentee situation, what might start as a useful and helpful relationship *could* develop into a 'father–daughter' or 'boss–secretary' relationship, rather than one that is colleague-to-colleague. If such roles are enacted, inevitably they will leave the female mentee feeling frustrated and dissatisfied. The traditional mentoring concept – in terms of the 'apprentice' or 'protégé' being 'watched over' by a 'wise senior' – clearly needs sensitive interpretation if paternalism is to be avoided.

Relevant to this point is the notion that males and females tend to bring different touches to jobs. No one wants to stereotype, but there is evidence that the male role tends to involve characteristics such as control, dominance, competitiveness or aggression, while the female role is sometimes assumed to focus on 'softer' traits, like cooperation, intuition, responsiveness or expressiveness. This raises the need for male mentors to be aware of possible differences in expectation about styles of teaching or pupil management or general professional behaviour when they enter mentoring relationships. A male mentor who tries to guide a female NQT by his values and strengths may find this conflicts with, and undermines, her preferred way of operating. It will do nothing for building her confidence as a new teacher.

Activity 6.2

Look at this list of words. They represent various attributes of effective mentors:

colleague guide appraiser protector motivator teacher consultant assessor listener helper diagnoser trusted guide reviewer facilitator counsellor expert challenger critical friend

Which ones:

- reflect features of your current role as a mentor?
- describe aspects of your role that you wish to develop in the future?

(Adapted from Capel et al. 1997: 33)

Chapter 7

Communication skills

Key issues

- *What are the skills needed for good listening and what are the barriers?*
- *What are the different types of questions that are useful for helping NQTs unpack and understand their classroom experiences?*
- *What kind of body signals should mentors be aware of during professional discussions?*

The effectiveness of the professional relationship that is developed between mentor and newly qualified teacher depends on the successful implementation of a number of generic mentoring skills. These include interpersonal, observational, assessment, target-setting and written skills, many of which place a strong premium on the mentor's *ability* to communicate. This chapter explores the key skill areas that mentors need to develop in order to support, supervise and nurture NQTs during their induction year.

Listening

Listening is a crucial element in enabling mentors to communicate with their NQTs. There are many occasions when they will want to talk about their teaching, their pupils, their problems and their ideas. Listening carefully will not only enable the mentor to hear what is said, but to understand it and to demonstrate that one is valuing the NQT as a person and a professional colleague. In meetings, particularly, the mentor must endeavour to be an effective listener if NQTs are to be offered the best possible advice and assistance for their future practice.

Effective listening is a vital skill, entailing hearing another person's words, thinking about their meaning and then planning how to respond – all very quickly! Focusing on significant issues and using verbal prompts to develop or clarify points are two ways of approaching it (see Reading 7.1).

On the other hand, there are a number of obstacles to effective listening that should be avoided (see Reading 7.2).

Reading 7.1

Focusing: In the early stages of the relationship, mentees may wander from the topic under discussion. They may have so many pressing queries and comments that it is hard for them to keep to one point. The mentor can help the mentee to focus by, for example, selecting one area of the conversation: 'Can you tell me which part of the lesson you felt went particularly well?'; 'What were your feelings as we've been talking about this incident?'

Verbal prompts: The mentor can encourage the mentee to talk more, to clarify a point, to extend a thought, by:

- using small sounds like 'Uh-huh' and 'Ye-e-s' and encouraging expressions like 'I see' and 'Go on...'
- repeating a key word (a technique borrowed from counselling skills); for example, if the mentee says 'I'm really anxious...' the repetition of the word 'anxious?' may prompt mentees to say more, and also assures them of the mentor's concentrated interest.

(Beels and Powell 1994: 16)

Reading 7.2

On-off listening: Most of us think about four times as fast as the average person speaks...Sometimes we use this extra time to think of our own personal affairs, concerns or interests instead of listening.

'Open ears – closed mind' listening: Sometimes we decide rather quickly that either the subject or the speaker is boring and what is said makes no sense. Often we jump to conclusions that we can predict what he/she knows or will say.

'Glassy-eyed' listening: We almost seem to be listening although our minds may be on other things...We drop back into the comfort of our own thoughts. We get glassy-eyed...We can tell when people look at us in this way. Similarly, they can see the same in us and we are not fooling anyone.

'Matter-over-mind' listening: We do not like to have our opinions and judgements challenged. Consequently...we may consciously stop listening or even become defensive and plan a counter attack.

Being 'subject-centred' instead of 'speaker-centred': Sometimes we concentrate on the problem and not the person. Detail and facts about an incident become more important than what people are saying themselves.

'Pencil' listening: Trying to put down on paper everything the speaker says usually means we are bound to lose some of it because the speaker's words come out faster than we can write them down. Eye contact also becomes more difficult.

'Hubbub' listening: Sometimes there are too many distractions when we listen – noise, movement of people or other matters clamouring for our attention.

(Haykin *et al.* nd: 19–20)

Activity 7.1

This activity will need to be done with another mentor, or any colleague, in your school. Ask the other person to describe a recent successful lesson, but before that he/she should write down the key points to get across. They should not be disclosed at this stage. Your colleague should then talk enthusiastically and in detail for three minutes or so about why the lesson went so well.

What you must do is pay close attention to everything you are told and, if necessary, ask questions about what you are hearing. Then relate back to your colleague what you felt were the most important elements of his/her talk.

In comparing your analysis with your colleague's key points, ask yourself the following questions:

- how well did I interpret the meaning of what I was told?
- what have I learned about my listening skills?
- what steps do I need to take to improve?

(Adapted from Acton et al. 1992: 17–18)

Questioning

Questions enable the mentor to ask for known information and to encourage the NQT to offer viewpoints and judgements and justifications. Effective use of questioning is essential if one is to tease out of NQTs what is going on in their minds and how they see the success or otherwise of their lessons. Injudicious use of questioning, on the other hand, will not encourage them to talk constructively about their experiences. Also, a new teacher might be worried about upsetting or annoying his/her mentor. One's status in the school might lead the NQT to give an answer that is 'correct', rather than 'true', in terms of his/her expectations of what should be said. All this will make it difficult to arrive at a shared diagnosis of current practice and prescription for improvement.

It is important, therefore, to guard against questions that are perceived as threatening, especially if the NQT does not feel confident and seeks to protect him/herself. One will need to note carefully how the person being spoken to is responding and to judge how far to proceed and when to call a halt. The style of questioning that one should adopt depends very much, therefore, on the individual teacher, the situation under scrutiny and the particular stage in the NQT's induction. However, it is possible to identify certain types of question that are likely to prove productive in the responses they elicit.

Reading 7.3

Open questions: They may be used to:

- gain information: '*What happened as a result?*'
- explore thoughts, feelings, attitudes and opinions: '*What were you hoping to achieve?*'; '*How are you feeling having done that?*'; '*What's your view on that?*'
- consider hypothetical questions and explore options: '*What would help?*'; '*How might you deal with . . .?*'; '*What are the possible options for . . .?*'

Closed questions: These invite a 'Yes' or 'No' answer and as such may unhelpfully close down the options for responding . . . [They] take the discussion along a downward spiral of awkward communication with the mentee saying less and less and the mentor becoming pressurised to ask more and more questions . . . There are times when closed questions are useful as a questioning summary: '*So, overall, you are saying you were pleased with that lesson?*'

Elaboration questions: These may or may not be open questions, and are used to encourage the person to elaborate on what has already been said: '*Can you give me an example?*'; '*Can you say a little more than that?*'

Leading questions: These suggest to the mentee that a particular answer is expected, and that there are particular beliefs or values that should be held: '*Do you really think that ...?*'; '*Shouldn't you be considering...?*'

Multiple questions: Several different questions are asked in one sentence leading to potential confusion for both mentee and mentor: '*Is it that you felt . . . or that you think it would be better if . . . or perhaps that she should . . .?*'

(Beels and Powell 1994: 17–18)

As stated above, the choice of question types will depend on the purpose of any one particular mentoring meeting. Then there is the questioning strategy decided on by the mentor. For instance, *funnel questioning* involves beginning with open questions and then narrowing the focus of the meeting to specific points. Probing for further details, of course, requires care, lest the probing ends up as prompting. *Pyramid questioning* starts with closed questions and then broadens out in its focus, thereby encouraging the NQT to expand on his/her attitudes and feelings. Some questions will produce inevitably confused responses if they are imprecisely worded, jargon-ridden or too wide-ranging.

Mentoring meetings held early in the induction year are usually supervisory in nature, involving guidance and support, supporting and building, encouraging the attainment of standards of performance, and reviewing progress and setting priorities. This will often involve a 'control' model of questioning and conversation because of the need to ensure the NQT effects an improvement in performance. Analysis of the ways in which control can be exerted enables one to identify what are termed the 'footprints' of supervision.

Reading 7.4

Enquiry without advocacy: in which the reason for asking is not disclosed, e.g.
Why did you choose that topic?
What were you trying to do when you?...

Advocacy without enquiry: making statements that require the other person to do something, but without checking whether they're understanding/able/ interested, e.g.
The school handbook says you should...

Unillustrated attribution and evaluation: which show that you've reached conclusions but don't disclose why, e.g.
I thought that was a successful lesson. What did you think?

Undisclosed and privately tested assumptions: these don't let the other person know what you are really getting at, e.g.
How is your record of observations going?
(while privately thinking the person hasn't done one).

(Wilkin 1992: 105)

By contrast, questions and conversations of a more supportive nature will involve the mentor in negotiating a shared agenda, providing rationales and avoiding making judgements without clarifying their basis. Where explicit attention needs to be given to bringing change and development onto the agenda, useful questions might be:

- what would you like to be different?
- what would be happening which isn't now?
- what can you do to bring this about?
- what steps can you take first?
- who needs to be involved in helping you?

It should not be forgotten that a pause or period of silence can be quite effective in eliciting further information or viewpoints from one's mentee, although it is important not to take it too far. Gillian du Charme, headmistress of Benenden, told the *Guardian* (11 November 1997) about her tutor at Cambridge, who was an almost sadistic user of the long pause. The don had the knack of asking difficult questions about her essays and, if she did not know the answer, would let the silence go on and on. It showed her an example she vowed to avoid in her teaching career!

Activity 7.2

Outlined below are three situations that a mentor could face. For each, work out some questions to show how you would proceed in the light of the NQTs' comments.

- On being asked how she thought the lesson had gone, a Maths NQT said 'chaotic'. The mentor, feeling that she tended to be pessimistic and too self-critical, thought it important to begin by looking at the NQT's achievements in the lesson.
- An English NQT's response to being asked what had gone well was 'Nothing – it was disastrous!' The mentor felt that the lesson's disorganised ending prejudiced his perception, so he began by focusing on those aspects that had gone well.
- A History mentor, concerned that her NQT has been vague about his aims for a lesson, asked how he thought the lesson had gone. His reply that he thought most of them understood what they were supposed to be doing brought home to her the mismatch in perceptions. So she asked the NQT direct, focused questions to enable him to see for himself some of the problems which she had observed.

(Adapted from Hagger et al. 1993: 56)

Body language

In addition to listening and questioning, there are some key principles to apply to a third form of communication between mentor and mentee, viz. the way in which one's bodily signals may wittingly or unwittingly have an effect on the other person in a meeting. People are not always conscious of the non-verbal messages they give out – and they can speak volumes! Outlined below are some of the ways we express ourselves with our bodies. Advice is given for helping NQTs avoid feeling a sense of hostility, confrontation or anxiety, thus encouraging them to maintain their sense of self-esteem.

Eye contact is probably the most significant form of body language because it implies recognition of some kind and can reveal a great deal about a person's true intent. Careful use of one's eyes will help attract and keep the attention of a mentee, whereas the use of fixed, glazed, withering or exasperated looks will invariably communicate feelings of unfriendliness, boredom, annoyance or impatience.

Non-verbal prompts like head-nodding or facial expressions provide evidence that the mentor is listening and may be used to encourage the mentee to continue speaking. Occasional nods indicate affirmation of the points being made by the other person, while facial expressions like raised or lowered eyebrows usually reflect sensitivity to his/her expressed views.

Body posture takes many forms and can exercise a powerful influence in meetings. Leaning slightly forward suggests interest or a wish to respond, while sitting back indicates that one's colleague is free to speak in an atmosphere of openness and receptivity. Slouching, on the other hand, is a sign of boredom or tiredness. Gestures with one's arms and hands betray emotions. They can convey a sense of defensiveness if they are folded and clenched; open palms reveal a sense of honesty and candour. Finger pointing and wagging should definitely be avoided. Wriggling one's foot implies irritation or impatience.

Choosing an appropriate setting also has a part to play in facilitating a positive discussion. A private and quiet room will help to avoid interruptions or distractions, thus indicating to the NQT the importance you put on your meeting. Use of easy chairs set at a slight angle will encourage a relaxed approach to the discussion and convey a sense of equality, whereas positioning oneself face-to-face from behind a desk poses a physical and psychological barrier for the mentee to surmount.

Activity 7.3

Watch a newsreader on television and see how he/she tries to keep viewers' attention by means of eye contact. Look at an interview or panel discussion and spot the signals the participants send out to each other via body language.

Chapter 8

Lesson observations

Key ideas

- *How frequently should classroom observations be carried out?*
- *How can mentors and NQTs establish a clear focus for observations?*
- *Who should undertake classroom observations of NQTs?*
- *What ground rules should be drawn up for the conduct of observations?*

Classroom observation is an integral part of the assessment of any newly qualified teacher. If the focus of the observation is sufficiently clear, it not only provides mentors with evidence of their strengths and weaknesses, but also offers a mechanism for helping new teachers improve and develop their teaching skills. A vital follow-up activity in this diagnostic process is the opportunity for feedback. It enables mentors to give advice about the best ways of improving knowledge and skills, as well as invite comments from NQTs themselves. Reviewing, linked to action-planning, is crucial in helping them gain a clearer understanding of what has – and has not – worked well, and how best to take things forward. The targets that are agreed for development often form a suitable focus for the next round of observation.

The Association for Science Education (ASE) has identified the following outcomes for lesson observations:

- present a systematic approach for increasing teacher effectiveness;
- offer a basis for making valid decisions regarding the teaching/learning process;
- establish a cooperative atmosphere for decision-making between the teacher and the observer;
- foster decision-making based on data that are recorded from the lesson rather than on the personal biases of the observer;
- make provision for enhancing teaching skills and changing teacher behaviour;
- be used with all types of teaching strategies, curriculum and materials;
- promote accountability on the part of both the teacher and the observer.

Informal observation and feedback will occur all the while as part of the day-to-day discourse between NQTs and their mentors. However, in setting up a formal routine of observation and review, it is important to establish certain guiding principles relating to:

- when classroom observations are going to occur;
- what the focus of observation will be each time;
- who will undertake the observations;
- how the observations will be carried out.

The first point to consider is the frequency of observations. During their initial teacher training school placements, NQTs were probably observed formally once a week. In their induction year, this need not occur so often in view of the fact that they have attained Qualified Teacher Status. A reasonable expectation would be once a month, although the frequency will hinge on the individual new teacher's competence and confidence.

Establishing a clear focus for observations is crucial. It is inappropriate simply to 'pop in' to a lesson to see how the NQT is getting on or to exercise a 'catch-all' brief and respond critically to whatever crops up in the lesson. The new teacher's initial progress and degree of confidence and awareness will be the key determinants in the early part of induction. He/she is likely to benefit, therefore, from observation of particular teaching skills, e.g. effective questioning, the presentation of key ideas and specialist terminology, or establishing a purposeful working atmosphere. These, and many other key competences, are itemised in the QTS and Induction Standards and constitute a useful bank of skills for mentors to draw upon in determining the focus for observation. This is not to say, of course, that one should avoid commenting on other aspects of the lesson or turn a blind eye to any problems not related to the agreed issue. Whatever the primary focus, it should be set in the context of the NQT's general teaching throughout the lesson.

If the decision about what to observe can be jointly agreed and take account of the NQT's enthusiasms or concerns, it will encourage active engagement in the assessment of his/her professional progress. Obviously, as the induction year progresses, NQTs should be encouraged to exercise greater responsibility in this respect. It is advisable, therefore, to have a pre-observation discussion about what can most profitably be observed.

Most NQTs prepare lesson plans, so a preliminary meeting will provide an opportunity to go through the lesson aims, how they are to be met, the degree of pace and direction to be employed, opportunities for differentiation etc. This makes sure that there is a shared understanding of the lesson content and the new teacher is observed in the light of his/her intended outcomes, not those assumed by the mentor. An ethical consideration for the mentor, in the event of a deficiency in planning, is whether to intervene at this point or let the lesson stand and diagnose shortcomings at the review meeting. Good teachers, of course, are responsive to stimuli from their pupils, so the plan should not be regarded as a rigid measuring rod against which the success or otherwise of the lesson will be judged.

Reading 8.1

The value of observation does depend considerably on having an agreed focus and on gathering as much detailed information agreed upon in advance...For example, if the agreed focus were on the directions given by the [NQT] to the class about the tasks they were to undertake, mentors might usefully have agreed in advance to collect information on:

- the situation within which the directions were given: that is, whether all the pupils were quiet and attentive;
- the exact words used in giving directions, and whether they were repeated;
- the immediate responses of the pupils...and whether or not these were noticed by the [NQT];
- how adequately, and by what means, the pupils were 'held' until the giving of directions was complete;
- opportunities for asking questions, and whether other pupils were listening to these questions and to the answers;
- other modes by which the directions were reinforced (e.g. writing on board, overhead projector or handout);
- indications, later in the lesson, of pupils knowing or not knowing what they were meant to be doing.

(Hagger and McIntyre 1994: 10)

The issue of who will undertake observations deserves consideration. The NQT's subject mentor will do most observations, but the senior mentor/induction manager also has a role. Other teachers in the NQT's subject department should be given the opportunity of bringing a 'fresh pair of eyes' to the observation process.

It is important to establish some ground rules for carrying out observations. Mentors need to think about how best to conduct themselves in order to make their presence as unobtrusive as possible. How will they be introduced, so that their presence is explained to pupils? Where will they sit? The common way is to sit passively at the back of the room with a report form so they can observe and record evidence. Sometimes, the 'cover' of doing some marking or sorting files in a corner is adopted. However, it can be advantageous to engineer participation, especially with individual and group activities, or even to work alongside as a support teacher. This kind of active observation requires a different means of gaining insight into the pupils' work and progress, since there will be no time for detailed notes. The approach used should be discussed and agreed beforehand, as should a procedure for coping with a serious disciplinary problem.

Two other issues to decide on are the use of a video camera and consultation with pupils. Videotaping parts of a lesson with a hand-held camcorder can be very helpful to new teachers in giving them an insight into how pupils see their actions, gestures and movements. Children's work and their comments about what they learned or found difficult in lessons provide another rich source of evidence.

Reading 8.2

- Ensure that you have a small notebook, preferably with carbon so that you may provide the mentee with a copy of your notes.
- Ensure that others will not interrupt the lesson on your account.
- Arrive before the pupils enter the room.
- Sit outside the direct line of vision of the teacher.
- Ensure you can see all pupils.
- Adhere to the agreed focus and objectives.
- Strike a balance between the need to secure adequate written notes and the need to observe teacher and all pupils.
- Avoid participation unless you have arranged a participating partnership or agreed that talking with individual pupils would be helpful.
- Remain for the whole of the agreed session.
- Thank the mentee and give a very brief oral comment.
- Reflect and feedback.

(Acton *et al.* 1992: 22)

The type of recording procedure used for observations is likely to have an influence on their conduct. Three broad styles of observation schedule have been identified by Furlong, Maynard, Miles and Wilkin, each of which have implications for the way in which lessons are evaluated. With adaptation, they are as follows:

Open-ended observation schedules (see Figure 8.1)

These lead the mentor to take a qualitative view that concentrates on particular aspects of generic qualities, like 'planning and preparation', 'classroom techniques' or 'professional qualities'.

Criteria-based observation schedules (see Figure 8.2a, b and c)

These enable the mentor to make a quantitative record of what has taken place in the classroom. They specify sets of skills and competences against which the NQT's lesson delivery can be assessed. This kind of observation instrument is more structured and has an obvious relevance to the current preoccupation with finely detailed teaching standards. The selection of a detailed focus for observation can be related to the particular stage of development an NQT is at during induction.

Pupil-centred observation schedules (see Figure 8.3)

These concentrate attention on the quality of children's teaching and learning experiences and their standards of achievement. Based on early OFSTED observation schedules, this approach is more suited for use later in the induction year when NQTs are less concerned with the minutiae of classroom practice and procedure.

PUPIL BEHAVIOUR	
Clear, consistent ground-rules identified	
Pupils follow ground-rules	
Watchfulness maintained on all parts of classroom	
Acts to pre-empt inappropriate behaviour	
Avoids confrontation	
Uses praise to promote positive attitudes	
Pupils sustain concentration	
Pupils are courteous	
Pupils work collaboratively	
Pupils show initiative and take responsibility	
FUTURE TARGETS	
NQT COMMENTS	

Signed: _____ [NQT]

_____ [Subject Mentor]

_____ [Induction Manager]

Date: _____

Figure 8.2a continued

Observation Focus 2: Subject knowledge, understanding and delivery

Name: _____ Department: _____

Date & Lesson: _____ Year Group & Set: _____

Indicators	Evidence-based judgements
SUBJECT KNOWLEDGE & UNDERSTANDING	
Lesson content relates to KS3 programme of study or KS4/5 exam syllabus	
Demonstrates knowledge and understanding of subject concepts/skills	
Builds on pupils' prior subject knowledge/skills	
Copes securely with pupils' subject-related questions	
Spots and remedies pupils' errors and misconceptions	
SUBJECT PLANNING & DELIVERY	
Identifies clear objectives	
Presents key ideas, using specialist terms and well-chosen examples	
Sets challenging class/group/individual tasks	
Caters for special learning needs, e.g. SEN/high ability	
Stimulates curiosity and enthusiasm for subject	

Figure 8.2b

Seeks to contribute to pupils' spiritual, moral and cultural development	
Appropriate use of texts, resources and ICT	
MONITORING, ASSESSMENT & RECORDING	
Assesses achievement of learning objectives	
Relates assessment to AT levels/end-of-KS descriptions/GCSE grades	
Uses variety of assessment methods	
Marks pupils' work, gives constructive feedback and sets targets for progress	
Uses assessment data to inform future planning	
Keeps records of pupil progress in line with school/dept policy	
FUTURE TARGETS	
NQT COMMENTS	

Signed: _____ [NQT]
_____ [Subject Mentor]
_____ [Induction Manager]
Date: _____

Figure 8.2b continued

Observation Focus 3: Effective pupil learning

Name: _____ Department: _____

Date & Lesson: _____ Year Group & Set: _____

Indicators	Evidence-based judgements
INDIVIDUAL PUPIL DIFFERENCES	
Shows knowledge of ways individual pupils learn best	
Matches subject matter and tasks to individuals' ability	
Creates opportunities to raise individual self-esteem	
LEARNING OPPORTUNITIES, GOALS & TASKS	
Defines learning goals	
Offers learning activities relevant to learning goals	
Uses differentiated learning strategies for groups and individuals	
Challenges pupils' thinking	
Provides opportunities for pupil interaction	
Assesses whether pupils have met learning goals and provides constructive feedback	
Teaches individual and collaborative study skills	

Figure 8.2c

WORK ENVIRONMENT	
Pupil seating/work place matched to learning activity	
Resources well organised and accessible	
Makes use of ICT	
EFFECTIVE COMMUNICATION	
Communicates learning objectives clearly and links to pupil activities	
Relates activities to previous/future learning	
Stimulates curiosity and enthusiasm for learning	
Communicates clear, sequenced instructions and expectations	
Makes effective use of questioning technique to provide pace and direction	
Listens to, analyses and responds to pupils	
FUTURE TARGETS	
NQT COMMENTS	
Signed: _____ [NQT] _____ [Subject Mentor] _____ [Induction Manager] Date: _____	

Figure 8.2c continued

NQT's name:	Class:	Date:

Content of lesson:

Quality of pupils' learning
(e.g. attentiveness, concentration, interest, attitude, understanding of purpose of task and how to do it, work effectively, information seeking, communicating ideas and information, applying knowledge and understanding, complete tasks, make good progress, evaluate work)

Grade _____

Standard of pupils' achievement
(e.g. quality of understanding, quality of written work, competence in key language skills, progress made in knowledge, understanding and skills, standard of work in relation to pupils' capabilities)

Grade _____

Quality of teaching
(e.g. expectations of pupils, clarity of learning objectives, activities chosen to promote learning, assessment of understanding and progress, suitable pace of work)

Grade _____

Signed _____ Overall lesson grade _____

Key: VG = very good, G = good, S = satisfactory, U = unsatisfactory

(Furlong et al. 1994: 62)

Figure 8.3 Pupil-centred observation schedule

Activity 8.1

Try using each type of observation schedule with NQTs in your school. What do you find to be the advantages and disadvantages of each type?

Whatever the style of observation used, it is as well to keep in mind the fact that classrooms are busy, public and unpredictable places!

Reading 8.3

- There is not enough time to focus on all events in depth.
- Events happen quickly and teachers make decisions quickly.
- Teachers develop routines for 'handling' classroom dynamics.
- Teachers and pupils can feel as though they are 'on stage'.
- Teachers direct most of their performance to an 'audience'.
- Teachers may behave in a particular way to an individual knowing there will be an effect on the rest of the audience.
- Even the most experienced teacher cannot predict classroom events with total accuracy.
- Internal and external disruptions and interruptions often occur.
- Teachers and pupils have strategies for coping with unpredictability.

(Beels and Powell 1994: 30–1)

Chapter 9

Reviewing and target-setting

Key ideas

- *What constitutes good practice in providing feedback for NQTs after classroom observations?*
- *How can target setting contribute to NQTs developing their professional practice?*

An essential part of classroom observation is the professional discussion that mentors should engage in with NQTs so that they can talk through what occurred in the lesson, give feedback, explore issues and identify targets for future action. The mechanics of when and how to undertake this review process is an important issue which sometimes assumes a secondary significance compared with the observation itself. In fact, it should be given comparable standing, in view of the contribution it can make to helping beginning teachers develop a clear grasp of the strengths and weaknesses of their subject delivery and classroom management. It is important, therefore, to plan feedback carefully so it can contribute to an NQT's professional development.

The first issue is timing. It is good practice to offer the teacher some brief informal comments immediately at the end of the observation while the events of the lesson are still very fresh in one's mind. NQTs invariably look for, and appreciate, a few words of constructive feedback and reassurance. There is, of course, a need to reflect critically on what has been witnessed before any formal, considered responses are made. Nevertheless, NQTs should be provided with a written copy of the observation schedule before the end of the next working day and a meeting should be arranged to discuss its content. To ensure this occurs promptly, times for the lesson observation and the review meeting should be agreed at the preliminary discussion. A decision could also be made regarding use of other kinds of evidence for the evaluation, such as videotaping, examples of pupils' work or feedback by the children about the lesson.

The second point to consider is how to structure the observation review meeting. It should be held in a venue that is quiet and free of interruptions. What is then discussed could be structured into three broad phases:

- teaching strengths observed during the lesson;
- possibilities and improvements;
- targets for future action.

It is essential to establish an appropriate balance between positive and critical comments. Mentors need to avoid the polar opposites of 'smothering with kindness' on the one hand and destroying the NQT with criticism on the other. Therefore, the discussion must be shaped in such a way that both positive and negative points are made constructively and supportively, in the interest of improving teaching performance. That is the way to nurture a spirit of open professional enquiry for classroom observation so that it is not seen as a threatening exercise.

First, the NQT should be encouraged to offer his/her thoughts about the lesson. Did it generally go well and what particular aspects were successful? Asking the NQT to pinpoint two or three strengths avoids the danger of the mentor starting off with a lot of talking. It gives the mentee the opportunity to offer some positive comments, thus avoiding a feeling of vulnerability. The mentor could then assist this initial morale-building phase by suggesting some additional strengths that were observed. Should there be a temptation to make sweeping judgements – such as 'the lesson was brilliant' or 'everything was disastrous' – the mentor will need to take the lead in directing the discussion onto the particular focus for the observation. Making reference to the teaching skills, competences or standards agreed upon in the pre-observation meeting will serve to generate more specific and thoughtful interpretations.

Case study 9.1

The focus of the observation in an English lesson had been the teacher's reading of a story to the class with a follow-up question and answer session. Mentor and teacher were in agreement that it had gone well, especially in comparison with a similar lesson two weeks earlier. The teacher was unable to identify why that part of the lesson had gone well, insisting that it had 'just happened'. For those skills to become part of the teacher's repertoire, it was important that she was able to identify them. The mentor therefore explained to the teacher that she had:

- read to the class in a clear voice
- varied her voice to make the story interesting
- scanned the class while reading
- asked questions of different kinds at a level the pupils could understand
- responded to pupil responses in ways that deepened their understanding of the story
- looked positive and enthusiastic

(Hagger et al. 1993: 57)

It is appropriate then to move on to aspects of the lesson which could have been approached in alternative and, possibly, more successful ways. Again, the NQT should be asked to offer suggestions, as well as receive comments from the mentor. The latter's ability to ask considered and probing questions is crucial at this juncture. If there are a lot of negative points, they must be prioritised so those germane to the agreed focus are addressed first and the new teacher does not feel overwhelmed. The mentor may need to give some directive feedback about weak performance. Ideally, agreement should be sought about specific aspects of classroom practice that could usefully be changed. When added to the agreed strengths, it puts the mentor and NQT in a position to arrive at a balanced, overall picture of the latter's performance. It also results in a shared agenda for future action and offers a possible focus for a subsequent lesson observation.

Reading 9.1

The skills of giving constructive feedback:

- be specific – neither positive nor negative feedback can be taken forward unless the recipient of the feedback is clear about what did or didn't work well;
- refer to evidence – observed behaviour or records;
- refer to agreed criteria – such as a set of competences or standards discussed, negotiated and agreed in advance;
- refer only to things that can be changed and developed;
- invite from the recipients their own comments on the focus of the feedback – their work in general, the observed lessons, the materials being discussed;
- it is important that you are honest . . . it is equally important that – where an observed lesson has been, in the new teacher's words, 'a disaster' – your sensitivity means that you will weigh up how much you need to say.

(Beels and Powell 1994: 37)

The final phase entails the setting of agreed targets. There is little purpose in evaluation if it does not lead to development. Target-setting, therefore, is an ideal means of clarifying those aspects of an NQT's teaching which have not worked well and could usefully be improved or changed. It may also relate to additional areas of professional practice to which the new teacher should be turning his/her mind. The process involves identifying clearly defined tasks or skills or competences for further learning, which should be challenging but achievable. Appropriately supported and linked to a time scale, they will provide momentum for the work of the mentor.

Reading 9.2

What are the benefits of targets? Targets provide:

- a framework within which motivation can develop;
- opportunities for the recognition of achievement;
- an opportunity to prioritise tasks and ensure the best use of resources;
- a clear focus for support, e.g. from other members of staff;
- a link between self-development and organisational development;
- a mode of working which should ease the transition into an appraisal system.

What is good practice in target-setting? Good targets:

- have been negotiated by mentor and mentee;
- are of consequence and are closely related to a shared competency list
- make demands on both mentor and mentee;
- are challenging but achievable in an agreed period of time;
- possess agreed criteria for recognising success;
- can be codified or abandoned to suit changing circumstances.

(Acton *et al.* 1992: 80)

Activity 9.1

Carry out a lesson observation and keep a detailed record of the particular learning experiences of one pupil in the class. In the review meeting afterwards, tell your NQT which pupil you monitored and ask for an account of his/her understanding of the kind of learning experience experienced by the child. Then outline your findings. There may well be different, as well as similar, perspectives identified.

Chapter 10

Critical self-reflection – meanings and intentions

Key issues

- *What are the various meanings and assumptions attributed to critical self-reflection?*
- *How can it help teachers improve technical and practical aspects of their work?*
- *What is its contribution to enabling teachers to consider the aims, purposes and values of the education system?*

Competences and standards have their part to play in providing a suitable framework for the induction and mentoring of newly qualified teachers. However, NQTs should be encouraged to engage in a scrutiny of their developing professional practice that is more profound than any skills-based model can offer. The ethos and priorities of a school are important to this approach, but the key to its successful implementation is the encouragement by mentors of a problematic, reflective appraisal of their new colleagues' teaching and learning practices.

As a generic concept, 'reflective practice' may be said to be a practical enquiry undertaken for the purposes of understanding and improving one's professional practice. It requires NQTs to focus on issues of immediate relevance in order to develop practical solutions *and* enhance their understanding of personally significant educational issues. It entails active, persistent and careful consideration of knowledge or belief in light of the grounds that support it and the consequences to which it leads. However, 'reflective practice' is not a unitary or straightforward concept in either its meaning or its use. It shifts according to the interests and interpretations of those using the term. So one must be careful about making assumptions regarding its implications for the teaching profession and teacher education.

According to John Dewey, the 'reflective practitioner' engages in active, persistent and careful consideration of any belief or knowledge. He said reflective habits and skills must be nurtured, and stressed the importance of 'continuous formation'. By this, Dewey meant people are forever participants in the process and, therefore, forever growing and reconstructing their professional experiences.

This strongly suggests that mentors can help new teachers address the many challenges they face by assisting them to explore their developing sense of 'self' in relation to their actions. It contains echoes of Jean-Paul Sartre's belief that we should always try to make ourselves what we *might* be.

Dewey was writing in the early 1930s. More recent theories and examples of practice found in the literature of reflective teacher education may be divided into three broad genres:

> Donald Cruikshank's *Reflective Teaching* (1987)
> Donald Schön's *Reflection in Action* (1983, 1987)
> Kenneth Zeichner's *Reflection as Critical Enquiry* (1987)

The model devised by Donald Cruikshank at Ohio University emphasises the analysis of one's teaching practice through something akin to a structured laboratory experiment. Intended essentially for student teachers, it involves their identifying forms of teaching that empirical research has judged to be effective and replicating it with a group of fellow-students. One then assesses the extent to which successful teaching and learning has occurred. The emphasis is very much on applying theory to a given teaching situation in order to make one's technical practice effective. Issues relating to appropriate ends are not at stake.

For Donald Schön, of the Massachusetts Institute of Technology, the 'knowledge-in-action' developed by the experienced and successful practitioner is more important than the work of researchers. Schön sees such knowledge as dynamic and situational; it becomes explicit through observation and reflection. By thinking 'on one's feet' or 'in the thick of things', one is engaging in 'reflection in action', although he recognised it is impossible for the process to be constant. He also states that one needs the chance to 'reflect-*on*-action', i.e. standing outside the day-to-day world of the classroom in order to examine practice after the event or practice in other contexts.

It is vital, of course, to be able to recognise what is problematic and then create a suitable context in which to respond. Schön labels this process 'problem setting'. The purpose is to change a situation from where it was lacking to a more desirable one, by means of experimenting, testing hypotheses and reflecting on outcomes. He urges practitioners to learn from what they do themselves, from being coached by experts (in the case of NQTs their mentors would fill this role) and from dialogue with other novices.

Reading 10.1

The study of reflection-in-action is critically important. The dilemma of rigour or relevance may be dissolved if we can develop an epistemology of practice which places technical problem-solving within a broader context of reflective enquiry, shows how reflection-in-action may be rigorous in its own right, and links the art of practice in uncertainty and uniqueness to the scientist's art of research. We may thereby increase the legitimacy of reflection-in-action and encourage its broader, deeper and more rigorous use.

(Schön 1983: 69)

Reading 10.2

Schön's theory of self-reflection is complex, yet it is based on a simple notion: that when a professional person reflects in action s/he becomes a researcher in a specific and particular practical situation. Because situations are complex and uncertain, and always unique because of the combination of variables which come together, practice problems are difficult to justify. They are also difficult to act upon, since judgement and action need to be taken to fit the particular characteristics of each case...The purpose of the action, in an activity like teaching, is to change the situation from what it was to a desired state, so that once action has been taken further management of information is required, to judge the effects of action and assess the newly created situation. According to Schön, this constant activity of appreciation, action, reappreciation, further action, leads to the development of a repertoire of experiences of unique cases, which are then available to draw upon in unfamiliar situations.

(Tickle 1989: 282)

The views of Cruikshank and Schön place a strong emphasis on the teacher's technical practice in *doing* the job effectively. It is an instrumental approach that does not extend to considering the broader contexts of educational goals or school structures. Inspired by Dewey, the concept of reflection offered by Kenneth Zeichner, of the University of Wisconsin-Madison, projects a more transformative perspective for the teacher. He says teaching and schooling need a reflective orientation that seeks to contribute to justice and equality. This will necessarily involve examining the aims, values and purposes of the educational system.

Zeichner draws upon Van Manen's conception of 'levels of reflectivity' in identifying three levels embracing different criteria. Each one is higher than the last and supersedes it in its purposes, although all are necessary and important for the teacher at different stages in his/her professional development (see Table 10.1).

Table 10.1 Levels of reflectivity

Technical rationality	Concerned with the efficient and effective application of educational knowledge for the purposes of attaining given ends. Neither goals nor the contexts of school and society are regarded as a subject for scrutiny.
Practical action	Goes beyond questions of technical competence to examine the values underlying practical actions and assess the worth of educational goals towards which an action leads. How are choices of practical action constrained and influenced by situational and institutional factors?
Critical reflection	Concerned with how moral and ethical issues impinge on the discourse about practical action. How can educational goals and experiences generally, and one's teaching specifically, contribute – or fail to contribute – to justice, equality and humanity?

(Zeichner and Liston 1987: 24–5)

In Zeichner's view, new teachers would be expected to transcend the immediate situation and imagine things as they *should* be. For Cruikshank and Schön, the question is mainly one of 'doing the job effectively'. This conceptual widening of 'reflective practice' takes it beyond questions of technical practice and classroom context to goals embedded in one's pedagogy and the curriculum and the school structure itself. It leads new teachers into the development of fresh perspectives about teaching and learning based on ethical possibilities.

There is a clear implication for mentors in all this. NQTs should be helped to develop their skills in classroom contexts, but it ought not to stop at technical issues. They should also be encouraged to develop an attitude of critical enquiry regarding their professional practice that leads them to think *critically*, not comfortably, about those contexts and their effects on the children who function within them. They should be helped to ask questions, to analyse and to consider alternatives within broader ethical and cultural contexts. The focus should be on what is '*possible*', rather than 'existing'.

Reading 10.3

John Dewey's arguments for educating the reflective practitioner...have not consistently been a part of the dominant discourse on teacher education... Teacher preparation programmes...have more often been based within the curriculum tradition Kliebard refers to as Social Efficiency...By the early twentieth century, a philosophy of scientific management was influencing the nature of work in business and industry. This philosophy was an argument for the need to break down the tasks of factory workers into small component parts and to train those workers to perform those tasks in the most efficient way possible.

Teacher educators adopted this idea from industrial management and adapted it...Research on teaching and learning came to be seen as the scientific way to objectively identify traits and tasks of an effective teacher. Prospective teachers could then be taught to perform those tasks and develop those traits. This utilitarian perspective was guided by an image of the effective teacher as one who performs particular tasks with expertise. Teacher education came to be understood as training in those behavioural tasks...

Our faith in the efficacy of the utilitarian discourse has been shaken by changes beyond both the school and educational research...Changing notions of the workplace are being reflected in arguments about the need to change school structure and practice. Long accepted notions of the efficiency of assembly line work have come under scrutiny and the talk of industrial organisation has shifted to arguments for a quality circle approach in which workers are encouraged to make decisions about how particular jobs might best be accomplished...Reflective practice, then, has emerged at a time when old faiths in industry and science have been weakened. As a slogan, 'educating the reflective practitioner' serves to convey...an image of change that teacher educators can rally around.

(Adler 1991: 146–7)

Activity 10.1

In placing teacher education within its broader historical and socio-economic context, Susan Adler makes a very significant point about the assumptions underlying the current preoccupation with competences and standards.

So reflect yourself on whether the Zeichner model offers possibilities for new teachers' professional development that go beyond the QTS and Induction Standards. Could most NQTs develop such skills of analysis? Could mentors provide them with the theoretical underpinning for a meaningful level of discourse? Or would they tend to restrict discussion to the practical knowledge base that informs reflection-in-action?

Chapter 11

The value of reflective practice for NQTs

Key issues

- *What is the value of critical self-reflection as a form of professional development?*
- *Can it help to bridge the division between educational theory and practice?*
- *What considerations must mentors bear in mind when creating opportunities for NQTs to engage in reflective practice?*
- *In what practical ways can it be used with NQTs to inform and improve their professional practice and thinking?*

Good teachers are constantly theorising without realising it. They do this by turning problems over in their minds, considering alternative solutions, testing their ideas on a trial-and-error basis and making thoughtful decisions about good practice. Informally, the process can occur several times daily as teachers consider whether they 'did the right thing' in this or that setting. Different approaches work for different people in different situations. It is this willingness to perceive and respond to specific situations in order to improve practice that underpins the models of reflective practice outlined in the previous chapter.

The first year of teaching, in particular, offers opportunities for reflection *in* and *on* action because NQTs bring into schools their emerging ideas about teaching and learning, based on their university/college courses and experiences on school placements. During induction they can continue to explore ways to teach and develop an awareness of the sort of teacher they wish to be. Some, of course, will proceed through the year relatively undisturbed because of their ability to manage classes and keep children enthusiastic and hard working. Nevertheless, they still need to have their existing ideas about teaching challenged and extended.

Regrettably, some experienced teachers deride this approach. They express a belief in the importance of the 'craft of the classroom' and a weariness with innovations. Background reading or looking for causal connections is seen as an expensive luxury, made irksome by the encoded nature of much research language. The National Curriculum, undoubtedly, has reinforced the notion of teachers as 'knowledge-deliverers', rather than 'knowledge-constructors'. Also, certain New Right sirens have dismissed 'theorising' as detrimental to good schooling. Its marginalisation in institutions of teacher training is regarded by some as part of the mission of successive governments to de-professionalise teaching in favour of 'down-to-earth' practice and 'common sense'. In that respect, Terry Eagleton's observation that 'hostility to theory usually means an opposition to other people's theories and an oblivion to one's own' contains a ring of truth!

The dichotomy between theory and practice is being partly bridged by the Teacher Training Agency's funding and publication of practitioner research. However, much of the gap is a matter of perception. The root notion of 'theory' is that of holding a perspective. It is the process of generalising from and about practice so that one 'intellectualises' experiences. As stated above, teachers *do* analyse their practice. It is the encouragement to articulate and share the principles underpinning it that still appears to be problematic and partly accounts for the tension. Increasing opportunities for critical self-reflection should demonstrate that systematic enquiry into practice can be mutually informative at both classroom and academic levels.

Mentors, therefore, have a key role in providing structured support for new teachers to bring their ideas and actions out into the open and subject them to professional discussion and scrutiny. Its importance must not be underestimated in terms of maintaining the problematic nature of teaching, rather than simply offering coping strategies and survival techniques. Hopefully, mentors will be laying the foundations for a career-long appraisal of classroom practices and beliefs, which is essential if teachers are to develop as creative, thinking professionals, and not remain mere functionaries. An intelligent professional, after all, is a person who is accustomed to reflecting on his/her practice, to regarding it as problematic and open to change, and to deliberating rather than asserting.

Reading 11.1

All practice has an underlying theory...and all theory must have some influence or potential influence on practice. Elliott (1989), in fact, claimed that teaching is research and the two cannot be separated. Carr (1995) argued the case for practice being an essential part of theory rather than just its testing ground... Common perceptions of their separate nature have traditionally resulted from the self-imposed status given to theory generated in academic institutions... and different uses of language to convey theory and practice...The development of partnerships between higher education institutions and schools, within the context of teacher training, offers a framework which addresses the link between theory and practice.

(Dann 1996: 34)

It is important, of course, to retain an awareness of new teachers' own concerns and priorities at the start of their careers. These often focus on practical issues concerning behaviour, classroom organisation, pupil relationships and how best to excite interest and motivation. Also, they sometimes have a sense of being swamped by the volume of demands, making them feel inadequate and threatened. If NQTs are to be encouraged, within the mentoring process, to engage in critical self-reflection and be active agents in their own learning, several important points must be borne in mind:

- **Time must be created.** NQTs sometimes have a sense of being swamped by the demands they face. Issues relating to educational theory and practice cannot be addressed during the lesson bell, while children file out of classrooms, or in the exhausted half-hour at the end of a hectic day. New teachers cannot be expected to read books or reflect upon educational practice over coffee. Self-reflection will have little value if it is just another hurdle to surmount during the induction year.
- **Help is needed with formulating a focus for reflection** Whatever area for reflection is chosen, it should be motivating, challenging and practicable. Some issues may appear idealistic, so assistance must be provided in making them legitimate targets to aim for in classroom teaching. The mentor's help in identifying and researching a manageable question, and then trying out possible solutions, will be crucial.
- **Build on and develop pre-existing beliefs** It is important to avoid smothering the perspectives brought of new teachers. Many feel obliged to make internalised adjustments to the traditions of their first school. A pluralist *regime* that generates space for individual contributions from teachers will welcome and nurture new perspectives. This is important, given the equalisation with which postmodernism regards the perspectives of all participants in any debate. It does not mean the NQT's view is 'correct' – only that it is his/her particular concern and so comprises a legitimate point for analysis.
- **Phase in the levels of reflectivity** At the start of induction, NQTs will be more receptive to opportunities for reflection that stress the technical aspects of their work. Put simply, surviving-and-coping is the initial priority for some! Once they have developed confidence in their basic teaching competence, they will be ready for a phase of reflection that offers them wider opportunities to evaluate their professional performance and contemplate the institutional and ethical ideals against which it may be set.
- **Be aware of emotional factors** This area is little researched, but it suggests that asking new teachers to inquire into their actions can affect their emotions. Any new understanding about learning, subject material or pupil behaviour relating to one's own teaching could lead to feelings of anxiety or inadequacy if the experience is negative. So NQTs need to be helped to develop an understanding of what is happening to them in order to manage their emotions.

These points highlight the importance mentors have in helping their new teachers reflect on the relationships between their teaching and their short and longer-term intentions. Reflective practice should enable NQTs to learn something of wider significance than basic standards of classroom delivery. Once these competences are being addressed confidently, the mentoring process ought to take them beyond self-evaluation of their teaching performance to more profound pedagogical issues, like how children learn effectively in any situation, and the social and ethical contexts of educational practice.

If opportunities for critical self-reflection are to be successfully created, NQTs need to define their own issues or problems, work toward practical solutions, and then reflect on the results and their viewpoints from a wider perspective. The cycle of 'action research' offers a very suitable vehicle for enabling them to observe, research, monitor and reflect on their actions. Like 'reflective practice', it is a generic term embracing a variety of strategies designed to result in improvements in some practical situation.

Reading 11.2

The teacher changes some aspect of his or her teaching in response to a practical problem, and then monitors its effectiveness in resolving it. Through the evaluation, the teacher's initial understanding of the problem is modified and changed. The decision to adopt a change strategy therefore precedes the development of understanding. Action initiates reflection.

(Elliott 1988: 28)

It is worth stressing again that the reflective practice cycle of plan, act, observe and reflect occurs as part-and-parcel of teachers' everyday work. All it involves is doing self-consciously what should come naturally! What is different is that teachers engaged in action research carry out such activities in a more systematic manner than normal, focusing on selected issues over a longer period of time. Furthermore, one's actual teaching constitutes much of the process of experimentation – the latter is not an isolated activity.

The experiential learning model adapted by Kolb and Fry provides a useful template for NQTs to use in collaboration with their mentors. They argue that learning, change and growth are best facilitated by an integrated process that goes through four stages. First, immediate classroom experiences are used as the basis for observation and reflection. They are then assimilated into a 'theory' from which new implications for action can be deduced. These serve as guides in creating new experiences that could be the focus for a further cycle of action and evaluation. Figure 11.1 represents the process.

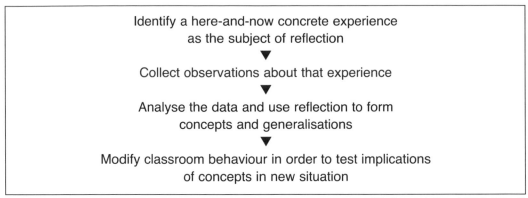

(Kolb and Fry 1975: 33–4)

Figure 11.1 Kolb and Fry's experiential learning model

There are numerous books on action research that take the reader through similar steps of critical enquiry. Table 11.1 below gives an outline of just a few examples of frameworks that mentors could use for their NQTs' reflective practice.

Table 11.1 Models of action research

Paolo Freire (1970)	• Observe and record everything in a chosen situation. • Share and critically analyse the data with whoever else is collaborating in the enquiry. • Structure a programme of action based on any contradictions identified in the analysis.
S. Adler and J Goodman (1986)	• Re-examine personal schooling experiences. • Consider what one's subject teaching should currently entail. • Use observations to record how it is actually taught. • Synthesise personal knowledge with information gained from reading and discussion with other NQTs.
John Smyth (1989)	• Write a narrative about a perplexing classroom situation. • Uncover the teacher's implicit theories in it. • Locate these theories in broader social and cultural contexts in order to re-evaluate taken-for-granted notions. • Reconstruct practice by considering alternative actions.

Whatever particular framework is used, following it through should serve to develop in NQTs skills and attitudes that are prerequisites for critical enquiry. A BEd course introduced in the late 1980s at the former Oxford Polytechnic (now Oxford Brookes University) was based on the development of a reflective teacher approach. During its implementation, the following skills, attitudes and values were identified:

Reading 11.3

Effective reflective practice fosters development of the ability to:

- work as part of a team;
- communicate and exchange ideas;
- observe using a variety of methods;
- analyse and evaluate data collected;
- develop micro-theories of action that, when organised into a pattern, represent an effective theory of practice;
- engage in self-assessment, peer-assessment and peer-teaching;
- seek out and examine alternative perspectives;
- develop attitudes that permeate the whole of one's personal and professional life;
- examine a conception of teaching and learning in which attention is paid to the social, political and economic context of educational decisions.

(Adapted from Ashcroft and Griffiths 1989: 36–7)

There is also an 'emancipatory' dimension to action research that is complementary to Zeichner's call for reflective practice to include the *contexts and ethics* in which teaching is embedded. It involves uncovering and understanding events in relation to dominant structural arrangements and changing factors that constrain equality and support hegemony. Like the notion of reflection as critical enquiry, it offers a transformative view of organisations and systems that is essential to cultivate if action research is not to remain at a superficial, technical level.

Reading 11.4

Reflective practice implies reflexivity: self-awareness. But such an awareness brings with it insights into the ways in which the self in action is shared and constrained by institutional structures. Self-awareness and awareness of the institutional context of one's work as a teacher are not developed by separate cognitive processes: reflexive, and objective analysis. Reflexive practice necessarily implies both self-critique and institutional critique. One cannot have one without the other.

(Elliott 1988: 50)

Everyone must start somewhere, of course, and some individuals will find some levels of research and reflection more accessible than others. Nonetheless, the new teacher will do little more than tinker with educational issues and problems if he/she remains at a technical, navel-gazing level. Basic assumptions about one's role as a teacher, expectations of pupils, the nature of what is taught, the principles underpinning how one teaches, learning theories, and the central aims and traditions of education are all likely to stay unchallenged if new teachers are not encouraged to ruminate over wider questions of institutional setting, the social role schools fulfil and the general values that govern the education system.

The development of this kind of reflective orientation in the induction and mentoring of newly qualified teachers depends very much on the individual school's *commitment* to its success. The school's ethos must lend itself readily to teaching within a framework of collect support and problem solving. There must be an enhanced culture of professionalism that encourages a critical approach to teaching and learning processes. That is what will create conditions conducive for NQTs to theorise about possibilities and reflect on their experiences. If more schools were to commit themselves to the active implementation of such a developmental and reflective ideal, they could claim, with a significant measure of justification, the title 'teaching schools'.

Activity 11.1

This activity enables mentors to offer their newly qualified teachers a structured opportunity to start reflecting on their actions and developing their perspectives on teaching and learning. It is targeted at the first two levels of reflectivity, viz. technical rationality and practical action, although there is the opportunity for participants to begin to relate their critical thinking to wider issues.

It is an exercise in the promotion of reflective practice that was piloted with a group of six NQTs in a secondary school. It was undertaken using the following steps:

- a personal tutorial with their mentor in identifying a broad area and then focusing on one aspect causing interest or concern;
- a four-week period during which they reviewed their existing practice, and then implemented and monitored a strategy for improvement;
- a further week in which to reflect on the outcomes and establish a 'claim' for improved professional practice;
- an afternoon symposium, during which participants made short presentations about their claims and took part in an evaluation of the project's usefulness and implications for professional development.

Key stages in developing reflective practice

1. Identify an area of professional interest or concern

Select an area of professional practice to act as your theme. You should discuss this with your subject mentor. The QTS and Induction Standards may well offer you an initial focus in the areas of:

- subject knowledge and understanding;
- planning, teaching and class management;
- monitoring, assessment, recording and reporting;
- other professional requirements.

2. Focus on one aspect that causes you interest or concern

Select one aspect or 'angle' that is professionally significant to you as an area of interest or improvement, e.g.

- do I have high enough expectations of pupils of high ability in my Y9 class?
- does my teaching in Y7 take sufficient account of the knowledge, skills and understanding that pupils have brought from KS2?
- do I employ teaching methods which develop a style of independent learning?
- do I give positive feedback to pupils in order to help them improve?
- do I use appropriate strategies that encourage positive behaviour?

3. Consider what you think you can do about it

Here you need to imagine possible ways in which you can exert a positive or improving effect on your selected aspect of current practice. You need to articulate your field of action by considering:

- what is my current practice like?
- why is it like this?
- what precisely do I want to improve?
- why is it professionally important to me?
- how could I go about this?
- what and/or whose assistance do I need?

4. Implement and monitor your strategy for improvement

Once you've got a clear plan in mind, with some 'imagined solutions', you can translate it into manageable action. The action you take should be documented carefully, so make sure you keep a record of your action, such as lesson plans, a logbook, an audiotape or a video. Conversational evidence from pupils and departmental colleagues will also prove useful. This will provide you with data for your evaluation.

5. Evaluate your research evidence

This is where you reflect upon the outcomes of your action. Questions to ask yourself include:

- has there been a practical change in my professional practice?
- have the outcomes any significance, and for whom and why?
- do I like the outcomes?
- what actual evidence supports my analysis?
- is it sufficient or could it be strengthened?
- have I engaged in a critical dialogue with any colleagues about my claim that improvement has taken place?
- can I contextualise my findings in any educational literature?
- how far can my action be related to wider issues of morality and equality in education?
- are there any constraints on my action, arising either within this school or in the education system on a wider level?
- have I developed professionally as a consequence of this exercise?

6. Establish a claim for improving professional practice

The final stage is to establish a claim about moving your professional practice forward in your chosen field of action (see Figure 11.2). It involves your making a brief written report and presentation to the other NQTs about what you claim to have learned as a result of your action. You need to be convincing about your claim – hence the importance of evidence. You also need to be critical about the criteria you've used to make judgements about what you are claiming as an improvement. This sense of 'moving forward' is your reflection on action.

Name	Department

The aspect of professional practice that causes me interest or concern is:

When I started, my practice was as follows:

These were the steps I took in trying to implement my improvement:

Figure 11.2 Claim for improving professional practice

This is the evidence I have used in making a judgement about my claim:

This is my evaluation of the success of my claim:

Response to claim

_____ [Mentor]   _____ [Date]

Figure 11.2 continued

Part III

The Management of Induction and Mentoring

Chapter 12

The school as a learning community

Key issues

- *What characteristics should a school display in order to be regarded as a 'learning community'?*
- *How will this contribute to an effective induction and mentoring environment?*

The development of induction and mentoring in a school can be either supported or undermined by that school's commitment to its success. Setting up, and then maintaining, a positive induction and mentoring culture is a key leadership and management role. It will contribute to the professional well-being and development of not only newly qualified teachers, but all staff. Successfully established and communicated across the whole school, it makes an institution what one head teacher described as 'a learning hive'.

The principal requirement is that the school should positively welcome the appointment of NQTs. Where they are seen as a necessary (and inexpensive) evil, to be managed – rather than developed – by a subject head and/or senior member of staff, in response to the umpteenth bullet point on a role specification, it is no wonder induction and mentoring are perceived as a burden! On the other hand, where NQTs are regarded as contributing freshness and vitality to the staff, one is likely to find induction and mentoring given a time and resource allocation that enables the appropriate post-holders to fulfil successfully their responsibilities. Invariably, the training process for NQTs is embedded in the school's general approach to professional development. Beyond this, a good mentoring school is likely to be one in which opportunities are available for *all* staff to benefit from a culture of enhanced professionalism. This is likely to be characterised by the encouragement of a critical pedagogical approach towards the nature of teaching and learning processes, and by a leadership and management style that thrives on discussion, collaboration and teamwork.

Some of the steps that a school's management should take, in trying to build an environment conducive to good mentoring, have been identified as listed:

Reading 12.1

1. They can subscribe to and defend a view of mentoring which is centrally concerned with support for... critical reflective practice...

2. They can insist that mentors play a full part in future school-based teacher education programmes. That is to say that mentors should not be limited to the assessment of classroom skills but should be concerned with the theoretical dimension and questions of values.

3. They can designate as mentors teachers who are themselves highly reflective professionals.

4. They can ensure that mentors have an adequate time allocation and realistic job descriptions so that they are able both to work with student-teachers and pursue their own professional development.

5. They can ensure that mentors are provided with substantial and extended support.

(Frost 1994: 141)

All these points, expressed within the context of student teachers on school attachments, would also enhance the mentoring provision offered to NQTs, ensuring it contributes to a climate encouraging a reflective approach to professional development and practice.

Research carried out by Keele University Department of Education – again in relation to initial teacher training – considered ways in which the successful nurturing of a mentoring environment depends on the three specific inputs: individual mentors, subject departments and the whole school staff. The authors, Derek Glover and George Mardle, argue that beginning-teachers' progression towards professional competence is most likely to occur when there is a supportive interaction between the subject mentor and other departmental staff and the school in general. They represented their findings as descriptors of contrasting positive and negative behaviour and attitudes on the part of mentors, departments and schools, although obviously a range of characteristics exists between these two poles. Also, in many primary schools, the whole-school and departmental factors usually merge into one (see Table 12.1).

Table 12.1 Elements of the training environment

	Supportive	Adverse
Mentor	Good role model with good knowledge of subject, challenging teaching style, good pupil and staff relationships, sympathetic but firm manner, insistence on standards, follows procedures and shows loyalty to others, commitment in time and effort, enjoyment of communication and counselling and monitoring activity, sees the [NQT] as a personal responsibility.	Poor role model with limited knowledge of subject, pedestrian teaching style, abrasive pupil and staff relationships, withdrawn or cynical, sloppy in procedures, ready to blame others, has little time for [NQT], sees work as a chore, little contact with [NQT] except when required by crisis or formal procedures.
Department	Team approach strong, see [NQT] as part of the team, share responsibility, assess the part each might play in support, evaluate on a regular basis, include the [NQT] in activities, share in planning and providing opportunities...	Function on an individual basis, see [NQT] as mentor's sole responsibility, not ready to cooperate in support, no part in planning or evaluation, see [NQT] as a nuisance but do as requested but no more, regard the mentor as paid for the job.
School	Has a strong system of shared values with whole school professional development and [NQT] policy known and understood. [NQTs] welcomed and integrated, developing professionalism recognised, valued as a source of new ideas and professional help, support in all aspects of personal and professional growth... build upon the development of competence and confidence.	...[NQTs] marginalised in staff room... may be critical of [NQTs] in front of pupils or other staff.

(Glover and Gough 1995: 140)

In their discussions with student teachers, the impact of the mentor was ranked as being of most importance, followed by the department. Those closest to an NQT, understandably, are perceived to have the most tangible influence on the mentoring environment. However, the influence of the school culture is also crucial. Glover and Gough tend to interpret school culture in terms of staffroom attitudes. However, a much broader definition will take into account reflective approaches to teaching and learning, a collaborative and consultative style of leadership and management, teamwork and communication, professional and personal relationships, and the extent to which school aims and policies are actually shared and put into practice.

It is this wider conceptualisation of a school's culture that will mark it out as a learning community – similar terms include Hargreaves and Hopkins' 'the empowered school', Holly and Southworth's 'the learning school' and Pedler's 'the learning company'. Michael Fullan amplified the idea in just a few words when he talked about such schools being occupied by 'continuous learners in a community of interactive professionals'. It implies an institutional climate in which high priority is given not only to pupils' development, but where also individual teachers are encouraged to learn and to develop to their full potential. In the jargon of modern-day business management, a 'human resource development strategy' is central to school policy. Hampstead School, in London, ably summarises this kind of approach in a simple statement of intent:

Reading 12.2

Learning Together, Achieving Together

At Hampstead School, everyone will strive to:

- enjoy the challenges and achievement of learning;
- develop individual strengths;
- experience academic, social and personal success;
- manage setbacks;
- develop consideration and co-operation within a stimulating and supportive environment and with the support of family and the wider community.

(Imison 1997: 11)

The idea of the 'learning community' needs a great deal more research and construction. Many schools may exhibit merely superficial features. Others will have in place many aspects of developing practice, while remaining unaware of the significance of the totality. There are different stages of development for schools to work through. Nonetheless, the benefits of such an institutional ethos and occupational culture for contributing to, and shaping, a successful mentoring environment are obvious. The evolving professionalism of the school's newly qualified teachers will be acknowledged and welcomed as a source of new ideas. Conditions will be conducive for them to reflect upon their purposes and experiences.

Activity 12.1

Try reviewing the current strengths of your present school as an environment for successful mentoring. How far do you think it is developing towards the concept of a 'learning community', in terms of:

- purposeful and participative professional leadership;
- shared vision and consistency of practice;
- core emphasis on quality teaching and learning;
- staff collegiality and collaboration;
- staff readiness to undertake professional development;
- staff engaging in mutual dialogue about professional practice;
- readiness to welcome new members of the profession;
- willingness of staff to take on a mentoring role;
- organisational transformation based on the outcomes of the above.

Chapter 13

The role of the induction manager/senior mentor

Key issues

- *What should be the roles and responsibilities of a school's induction manager/ senior mentor?*
- *What responsibilities will head teachers have to discharge under the DfEE's new induction arrangements?*

The process of offering and coordinating the widest possible experiences for the NQT is very demanding. It invariably calls on the services of more than one person, except in the smallest of schools. Research undertaken in recent years in a variety of school settings, such as the NFER survey of induction provision, distinguishes two broad types of mentor: the *induction manager/senior mentor* and the *subject mentor* (in secondary schools) or *classroom mentor* (in some primary schools).

The purpose of this chapter is to explore the roles and responsibilities of the induction manager/senior mentor. It is an appropriate brief for senior members of staff by virtue of their ability to influence and direct policy and action, which is why it is rare for teachers of more junior status to occupy the post. They can make sure induction and mentoring are treated as key aspects of school policy and practice. Other important contributory factors are the depth and breadth of knowledge and experience, overall view of the curriculum, general whole-school perspective, and respect from staff colleagues that he/she will possess. They should be well versed in dealing sensitively with the needs of adult learners.

Reading 13.1

Four out of the five schools investigated had structures involving the management of induction being the remit of senior staff. One was a deputy head and three held allowance posts carrying four points. Clearly, existing status was an important factor in their selection, as well as contractions in the number of deputy headships:

'I became the senior mentor by accident. The SMT shrank to two deputies, so some responsibilities were off-loaded when I was looking for a whole-school role in addition to being Head of Science.'

However, in another school a teacher in a Standard National Scale post, albeit of many years' experience, was induction coordinator as a result of several senior staff leaving at the same time:

'The lady in charge of NQT induction left. There was an obvious gap and I think because of the various pastoral roles I've taken on, people saw my experience as being of use. I was asked to fill in.'

Three induction managers had held their responsibility in its present format for no more than two years, which would suggest investment in the role is a fairly recent construct within management thinking.

(Bleach 1995: 36–7)

Apart from some primary schools, head teachers are generally not involved as they have usually delegated the induction manager's role to a deputy head or senior teacher. With the introduction of the DfEE's new induction arrangements from September 1999, that may well change. Head teachers are charged with measuring NQTs' performance against the QTS and Induction Standards, and then recommending to LEAs whether they should pass, fail or have their induction period extended. In addition, the following specific functions are identified for heads:

- ensuring each NQT has a mentor or induction tutor;
- putting in place a programme of monitoring, support and assessment based on each NQT's Career Entry Profile;
- allocating NQTs a timetable that is 10 per cent lighter than those of established staff;
- ensuring assessment procedures are rigorous and fair;
- observing NQTs who are in danger of failing;
- providing NQTs with a mechanism for raising any concerns about induction;
- keeping their governors briefed about induction arrangements.

There is an additional, wider role for heads in terms of giving induction and mentoring a whole-school credibility and commitment. Research into the mentoring of articled teachers in primary schools (carried out in 1990–92 by Pie Corbett and Diana Wright of Cheltenham and Gloucester College of Higher Education) identified the following issues for head teachers:

- there is a crucial role to play in developing a whole-school mentoring culture;
- they have responsibility for devising training opportunities;
- there is a clear need to ensure that new teachers' concerns are articulated and responded to;
- the development of new teachers is inextricably linked to the development of mentors and of the school as an institution;
- time is needed to develop various aspects of mentoring, such as assessment.

They also found that primary heads played a key role in the relationship between new teachers and mentors, particularly where difficulties were encountered. In such situations, the head acted as a 'sounding board' for both parties in an effort to resolve tensions and devise a way ahead. As well as helping to air problems, they provided 'cover' so that the teachers and mentors had time to meet to negotiate problems.

The principal requirement for an induction manager/senior mentor is to be responsible for the overall management of induction, i.e. the process of initiating the NQT into the profession in which he/she is newly qualified and the school organisation to which he/she is newly appointed. This entails not only a coordination role, but also monitoring and evaluation of the programme. It embraces various generic tasks, such as:

- organising a central programme of induction;
- undertaking individual interviews/tutorials with NQTs;
- the formative and summative assessment of their teaching performance, including lesson observations;
- coordinating the activities of staff designated as subject and classroom mentors;
- overseeing the NQT's induction entitlement (e.g. not being used for 'cover', release time);
- assuring the quality of the induction programme.

What comprises an appropriate agenda for an induction programme is explored in Chapter 15. Suffice it here to observe that the induction manager/senior mentor needs to ensure its content is broad enough to cover teacher roles that are distinct from issues of subject competence, e.g. classroom and behaviour management, voice care, child protection, special needs, assessment and report-writing, role of the form tutor, meeting parents, and so forth.

Coordinating the work of subject mentors is a priority to ensure that practice and supervision are consistent in different departments. Research shows the degree of frequency and formality varies in the way that senior mentors work with subject mentors. Where it is poor, mentoring ends up being perceived as a 'bolt-on', administrative and paperbound task, rather than an integral part of a coherent professional development programme. Research at Keele University points to the increasing importance of the latter, with its possible emergence as a third key dimension in the work of schools, alongside curriculum and pastoral areas. An example is shown in Reading 13.2.

Reading 13.2

Increasingly, professional mentors were taking a view of themselves as leaders of a team of mentors within the school. Where this was the case, the professional mentor had ceased to be merely organiser and administrator and had assumed the role of facilitator, professional developer and quality controller of the teacher education process in the school. The management of the team of subject mentors involved the professional mentor in establishing the team, providing an induction programme, and developing, maintaining and supporting the team...

The professional mentor was the appropriate person to convene regular meetings of the mentor team which would serve to establish an atmosphere of openness in the school with those directly involved in the mentoring process, and at which they could discuss the important points of their training and their implications for the school.

(Johnson 1995: 92–3)

There is a need for liaison with one's LEA, given the DfEE's requirement that local authorities act as 'appropriate bodies' in validating the successful completion of the induction year by NQTs. The post usually involves having additional charge of initial teacher training provision, requiring one to act as the point of contact with universities and colleges. It may also entail a wider responsibility for other staff development activities, like INSET, appraisal and Investors in People, which is likely to have favourable implications for the training opportunities of all staff.

Undoubtedly, the influence and negotiating skills of senior staff – and the power of effective action, where appropriate – are crucial factors in enabling them to give NQTs access to a rich and varied induction programme. The value of a high proportion of non-contact time in the mentoring of individuals speaks for itself. Their status and authority, coupled with access to all aspects of their school's work, is a crucial element in ennobling induction and mentoring with a high profile across the school, and in ensuring all staff understand how crucial it is to the concept and culture of a 'learning community'.

Activity 13.1

Schools should give careful thought to how they operationalise their mentoring provision, particularly in terms of who is appointed to take on the role. Whatever procedures individual schools adopt, it is likely there will be a broadly common view on the mentor's roles and responsibilities.

Using whatever format your school employs, draw up a role specification for the induction manager/senior mentor. It should reflect the kind of good practice identified above, as well as the existing post-holder's current responsibilities.

Chapter 14

Selecting and training mentors

Key issues

- *What criteria should be used for the selection of classroom and subject mentors?*
- *How can the professional development and training of mentors reflect the complexities and demands of the role?*

In secondary schools, most mentors are found within the NQT's subject department, while in primary schools they usually act as classroom mentors. Whatever their location, they have a crucial role to fulfil. They should be special people with whom new teachers can share concerns and needs. It is essential, therefore, that mentors are equipped with an appropriate profile of skills, qualities and experiences. Not every teacher is capable of mentoring – suitability, not availability, is what should determine who mentors.

Reading 14.1

The subject mentor inducts the [NQTs] into the department and into subject teaching. He or she has responsibility for developing... specialist subject knowledge, skills and application. Since there is a strong emphasis on developing... classroom competence, the subject mentor arranges a programme of observation, discussion and... teaching designed to introduce [them] to the range of teaching styles and practices within the department. It is usually the subject mentor who has the closest and most regular contact... and deals with their development and needs on a day-by-day basis.

(Brooks and Sikes 1997: 45)

In many secondary schools, subject mentorship 'goes with the job' of being a head of department. Often, responsibility for NQTs is included in the role specification. Indeed, some department heads believe they are the only ones who can do it by virtue of their management experience and subject knowledge. Mentoring can bring pressures, however. So sometimes it is delegated to another colleague as part of a departmental role distribution. This may be done for one of several reasons:

- in recognition of a teacher's years of classroom experience;
- as an additional outlet for energies;
- as a means of furthering career development.

Whoever acts as the named post-holder, what is vital is that the whole department should be positively involved in supporting its newest member. The qualities appropriate for effective mentoring are rarely the exclusive gift of one person!

Some schools deploy recently qualified teachers in a 'buddy'-type role. This is usually done within a structure that also involves the head of department and induction manager, thereby retaining the benefit of length of experience. Its merit lies in the 'recency factor' of being better placed to empathise readily with queries and concerns that might be regarded as trivial by higher status staff. An NQT is less likely to feel ill at ease in sharing such issues with someone who is close in age and has recently completed an induction period. Also, they may be more open to new ideas and ways of working than older staff. Certainly, the ability to retain a fresh memory of potential pitfalls, and to offer advice about avoiding them, is advantageous in cementing a professional relationship. There is evidence that new managers in other professions rank peers as the most helpful and accessible type of mentor when they are settling in to a new position. However, it is unlikely that such 'buddies' would carry sufficient authority to facilitate aspects of the novice's professional development.

Reading 14.2

The common belief that a mentor should be an 'experienced' teacher was not a view that our experience confirmed. It seemed that mentors who had only recently completed their own training might be well placed to become part of a partnership in learning. In these circumstances, mentor and articled teacher could observe for each other, discuss difficulties as they arose, share and use each other's strengths. Several such partnerships were formed where both parties learned and developed together. In one school, both mentor and articled teacher had previously been employed in industry; a significant strength of this partnership was their common experience of appraisal and regular target-setting – this was reflected in a comprehensive and professional training log.

(Corbett and Wright 1993: 225)

The usual expectation is that anyone selected for mentoring will be an experienced individual who is an effective and credible teacher. There are obvious risks in appointing somebody who has yet to establish a good track-record, in view of the way that he/she may be regarded as a role model. Even then, being an excellent teacher is not a sufficient qualification for mentoring – a point recognised by OFSTED when it required schools to demonstrate 'clear procedures' for identifying teachers who would act as mentors in ITT. Particular perspectives, attitudes and skills are needed in responding to the needs of adult learners if one is to take advantage of the range of experiences they bring to teaching and if they are to be successfully guided in developing their own styles of teaching.

Various research reports on school-based ITT, published over the last five or six years, have identified criteria for the selection of subject and classroom mentors. Through constant definition of the role, a detailed picture has emerged of desirable attributes. They include, among many others: wide educational experience, a good professional reputation in the school, the willingness to give time to others, competence in the skills of mentoring, the ability to recognise one's own developmental needs, and being appropriately trained for the role. Two examples are given in Readings 14.3 and 14.4.

Reading 14.3

Role model qualities:

- a suitable, adaptable, sympathetic, understanding personality;
- reliable, conscientious;
- articulate;
- has an interest in their own evolution.

Guidance and counselling skills:

- good interpersonal skills;
- supportive;
- accessibility.

Knowledge/experience:

- teaching and academic ability;
- philosophical grasp of mentoring;
- experience of teaching;
- experience of working with trainee teachers;
- interest in information technology.

(Devlin 1995: 66–7)

Reading 14.4

Effective mentors should have experience and expertise in, for example:

- enabling individuals to learn in the ways that are most effective for them;
- ways of managing and organising classrooms;
- planning and developing curricula;
- matching content and pedagogy to the pupils they teach;
- dealing with difficult pupils;
- a range of marking and assessment, recording and reporting techniques;
- planning and managing practical work, where appropriate;
- working collaboratively with colleagues.

A mentor's personal characteristics and their interpersonal skills and qualities are obviously important, as is their professional commitment. Mentors should:

- be enthusiastic about teaching;
- be willing to reflect on their own practice;
- be able to articulate their professional knowledge;
- be open-minded with the view that their approach to teaching and learning is not the only one, nor indeed the 'best';
- be willing to develop their own skills in, and understandings of, teaching and learning;
- be accessible, with a sympathetic and understanding approach to [NQTs];
- have a positive and encouraging attitude;
- have the ability to be critical in a constructive manner;
- be a good communicator and a good listener;
- be committed to their role as mentor;
- be aware of relevant educational theories and be able to relate these to their practice.

(Brooks and Sikes 1997: 67–8)

Mentoring is certainly a complex role! These two lists of criteria, alone, present a challenging list of professional and personal attitudes, skills and qualities, against which potential mentors will feel they must pass muster. Nonetheless, in schools up and down the country, teachers are working hard at doing their best because they value mentoring as a means of inducting fresh and enthusiastic new colleagues into the profession. It also has a tonic effect: they do it because they recognise the rewards to be gained from exercising a responsibility for the development of others. And they see the potential beneficial impact of the exercise on their own teaching practice, their work satisfaction and their career development.

Reading 14.5

The reasons given for staff to show such readiness to accept the extra responsibility varied from individual to individual. For some it had to do with investigating the possibility of a move into teaching in the HEI... There was certainly seen to be career advantage in the development of transferable administrative, organisational and managerial skills demanded for the role... For others it was to do with diversification at a time when they needed a career move [in order to provide] a whole new perspective and a different set of relationships. For some... it was simply to do with enthusiasm for influencing the next generation of teachers.

(Johnson 1995: 86)

Part of the success of any mentor's work depends on having received some form of in-service development. For any school that takes seriously the notion of staff development, it should be regarded as every bit as much an entitlement as the induction training received by NQTs. Mentoring *is* different from what seasoned teachers have always done to help probationary teachers, particularly if one is aiming to nurture reflective young practitioners who are competent in the use of a variety of teaching strategies. Use of focused observation to see someone teach, then reviewing it in an evaluative, helpful manner and setting targets for development *does* require training. Also, it cannot effectively take place without some understanding of the wider aspects of mentoring.

So how should one set about this inevitably varied and individual task? Just as there is not a single model of mentoring or definitive list of mentoring qualities, it follows that effective training offered by schools or by external agencies should assume a number of forms.

- Helping the NQT continue to develop his/her skills as a subject teacher is one key area. It implies a strong pedagogical role for mentors in terms of demonstrating adeptness in the analysis and articulation of principles underpinning how their subject is taught. This does not apply only to secondary schools. The re-emergence of a subject-specific curriculum in primary schools raises a particular question for schools in that phase regarding who will provide the necessary subject guidance. Secondary-style subject specialism may not sound the death-knell of the generalist teacher, but it does means primary mentors must offer greater support for NQTs to become good teachers of their particular subject(s).
- A second crucial area involves ensuring mentors have sufficient information and skills to assist their NQTs with general classroom practice. Examples of this include good pupil-teacher relationships, preparation of lesson plans, use of a variety of teaching and learning methods, monitoring and assessment, record-

keeping and reporting classroom organisation, preparation of resources, pupil administration – and much, much more! The QTS and Induction Standards provide a comprehensive framework for addressing this need.

• Thirdly, it is necessary to focus on the development of good interpersonal and counselling skills if one is to encourage NQTs to be as candid as possible about their experiences and difficulties. Mentors need assistance, for instance, in the effective use of communication skills like observation, listening and giving feed-back, motivation and confidence building, supporting new teachers who have personal problems and representing their interests with other colleagues. When dealing with the affective dimension of mentoring relationships, very often a style of INSET that involves problem-solving and simulation exercises is most appropriate. It is more likely to guide mentors in structuring an exploration and exchange of views, and clarifying ways forward, that could be applied to particular situations.

Many schools have a well-established tradition of in-house training and possess sufficient knowledge and experience among their staff to make adequate provision in the above three areas. It should not be forgotten that universities and colleges of higher education have run mentor training courses for school colleagues in ITT partnerships, so many of the lessons acquired on these are easily transferable to the induction of new teachers. The fact that some universities have also launched Post Graduate Certificate courses in mentoring is a further step in ensuring mentors are provided with the necessary knowledge, experience and opportunities for reflection that they need to make a success of their role.

With the DfEE's re-introduction of a role for local education authorities in applying common quality standards and expectations regarding induction across their schools, logically they will also have a future part to play in the training and support of mentors. Courses organised in the past by LEAs have put an emphasis on observational methods, interpersonal skills and engaging NQTs in discourse, as well as providing mentors with guidance documents and opportunities to meet each other and engage in critical debate about their approaches and difficulties.

Activity 14.1

Assuming that suitability, rather than availability, is a feasible yardstick to apply in your school, how would you, as a senior manager, go about selecting either subject or classroom mentors? If you had to draw up a role specification, what would you put under the following sub-headings:

• status (should it be a head of department or another member of staff?);
• professional practice (what qualities make for a good role model?);
• personal qualities (what will contribute to the 'feelings' aspect of working with NQTs?).

Three key areas of mentor training are identified as:

- subject teaching;
- classroom practice;
- interpersonal skills.

Think about the extent to which your school could successfully make provision for mentors. If not, how would you seek to supplement in-house courses by making use of external bodies?

Chapter 15

Policies and programmes

Key ideas

- *What should be included in a school policy statement on induction and mentoring?*
- *What constitutes effective induction?*
- *What are the key professional issues that should be covered in a school induction programme?*
- *How can schools identify and respond to NQTs' individual training and development needs?*

A school policy on induction and mentoring

Managing all the interrelated aspects of a school requires a complex arrangement of working systems shared by those who are doing the job from day to day. Developing a school policy statement on a key issue – like induction and mentoring – needs to be done in a planned way, based on a practical under-standing of what constitutes good practice. This should allow decisions to be made and procedures to be followed quickly, consistently and effectively by reference to agreed principles. It also gives a clear picture of what is expected of everybody who is involved:

- how NQTs can make the best use of the opportunities offered during induction;
- what procedures subject/classroom mentors, and other subject staff, should follow in supporting and assessing NQTs;
- why the senior management team regards induction and mentoring as a crucial and beneficial activity for the school.

A policy statement, therefore, will be testimony to a whole-school commitment to induction and mentoring in the long term, offering staff a shared understanding of its purposes and of the responsibilities of everyone who contributes to, and benefits from, the process. In this respect, Johnson and Scholes' work on corporate strategy is relevant, in which they refer to business decisions being based on feasibility, suitability and acceptability. Applied to a policy decision committing a school to an effective programme of induction and mentoring, as Brian Fidler has attempted to do, it could be framed around these three criteria as follows:

- feasibility – the school's long-term commitment to induction and mentoring when set alongside other strategic priorities;
- suitability – the school's perception of the DfEE's new induction arrangements as either an opportunity or threat, and its assessment of its own capacity to respond as an institutional strength or weakness;
- acceptability – whether the potential stakeholders in the process (department heads, SMT, governors) will support it in order to make it a success.

The format adopted by schools for policy presentation varies considerably. It is inappropriate, therefore, to offer templates, except to suggest that it would be good practice for policies to be drawn up under the two broad headings of 'purposes' and 'procedures'.

The 'purposes' section should comprise a brief statement relating the policy to school aims or the mission statement, so it can be shown how induction and mentoring specifically contribute to their implementation. This section should also itemise induction and mentoring's principal benefits and outcomes for NQTs, mentors and the whole school community.

The 'procedures' section should give details about how the policy is put into practice, e.g.

- roles, responsibilities and working relationships of the induction manager/senior mentor, subject mentors, classroom mentors and any other staff who are involved;
- training needs and induction programme;
- lesson observation, reviewing and target setting;
- mentoring and counselling provision;
- assessment, 'at risk' and quality assurance arrangements;
- where appropriate, partnership arrangements for ITT school placements.

Some schools develop policies once systems have been put in place, while others use policy statements to initiate structures. Also, there are differences in the degree of staff involvement: policies can emerge as papers devised by a staff working party or as drafts prepared by one person, which are then presented to a wider audience for consultation and amendment. A procedure should be included for monitoring, reviewing and evaluating the policy to see that the school's published intentions are indeed being met.

Figure 15.1 is an example of a 'statement of entitlement' for NQTs in a secondary school. It sets out school aims with regard to new teachers, the commitments they are offered and the school's reciprocal expectations. It formed the starting point for a much more substantial school policy statement, which was subsequently developed in anticipation of the DfEE's new induction arrangements.

Sneyd Community School, Walsall

Statement of Entitlement for Newly Qualified Teachers

At Sneyd Community School we aim to provide all Newly Qualified Teachers (NQTs) with the opportunity to:

- gain experience of working with children in classroom and wider school settings
- gain experience of school and faculty organisation
- observe experienced teachers at work
- gain experience in the teaching of individual pupils, groups of pupils and classes
- develop essential confidence and the capacity to establish a learning environment
- develop skill and understanding in the area of classroom management and control
- demonstrate the ability to work harmoniously with children and colleagues
- gain experience in the planning, execution and evaluation of individual lessons and schemes of work
- develop sound and competent teaching strategies
- provide a commitment to teaching as a career choice.

To these ends, we pledge to offer NQTs the following commitments:

- a two-term period of probation as a condition in the contract of employment, with one term's extension if, in the opinion of the School Governors and the LEA Chief Inspector, there is any doubt about an NQT's proficiency
- the provision of a teaching load lighter than that of an MPG teacher and the protection of all non-contact periods (where possible) in the first term
- a timetable that will offer teaching experience across a range of age and ability
- formal lesson observation by the Subject Mentor at least once every half-term, with a written appraisal, prompt follow-up discussion and target-setting
- monthly review meetings with the Subject Mentor that focus on the NQT's progress within the context of the QTS Standards
- a meeting with the Senior Mentor every half-term to discuss their development and set future targets, to formulate their own perspectives on teaching and learning, and to develop an extended professional view of educational issues
- a meeting with the Head teacher every term to discuss the NQT's LEA report
- to carry out an audit of each NQT's competences and needs in order to plan relevant and differentiated INSET in the first two terms
- to enable NQTs to observe teaching by more experienced colleagues
- to organise observations in local primary and secondary schools
- to use funds delegated by the LEA for NQT induction to finance supply cover for suitable courses and observations, professional development materials, etc.
- to offer a professional development continuum into the second year of teaching.

Figure 15.1 Statement of Entitlement for NQTs

In reciprocation, we hold the following expectations of NQTs:

- to take the initiative in seeking advice and help from the Subject and Senior Mentors with any matters relating to their personal and professional welfare
- to be well prepared for teaching lessons and have lesson plans readily available
- to act upon the constructive comments of staff who observe lessons
- to observe more experienced teachers in the home faculty, elsewhere in the school and on visits to other schools, in order to learn from their good practice
- to take full advantage of the school's induction programme
- to engage in reflective self-analyses of their professional practice and the underlying assumptions on which they are based
- to play an active part in the everyday life of the school by fulfilling administrative and pastoral responsibilities and school duties
- to maintain the school's professional ethos in terms of appearance and conduct.

Figure 15.1 continued

Activity 15.1

Now try writing a draft policy on induction and mentoring for your school, taking into account its style of policy presentation. The policy statement should express a commitment to, and understanding of, the role and purpose of induction and mentoring. It should proceed to specify various aspects of the structure and system in operation, with explicit guidelines given for the work and expectations of all staff involved, from senior mentors to subject/classroom mentors to NQTs (and ITT students, if appropriate).

Effective induction programmes

In the early 1990s, the NFER's research project on induction – covering 30 schools and six LEAs – found that programmes deemed to be effective seek to provide new teachers with the kind of support and guidance that will help them effectively fulfil their professional duties. They also act as a starting point for subsequent training and development. Induction managers who were asked for their views on effective induction expressed the aim of trying to ensure that their NQTs felt happy and confident, regarded themselves as valued part of the school team, and sought to contribute both to their own development and that of their school.

A strong emphasis was put on providing NQTs with the opportunity to negotiate some of the content of induction courses, rather than offering a solely pre-determined input. Giving them an active role would ensure induction was sufficiently flexible to recognise their individual needs, researchers were told, rather than being something that was simply 'done' to them. This would help foster a climate in which new teachers felt confident about sharing concerns regarding any problems or weaknesses. Where this worked, it was usually symptomatic of a general ethos of mutual support between staff in the school.

Systems of support and development were also important. These manifested themselves in features like the allocation of a personal mentor, schedules of classroom observation and feedback, and the chance to meet regularly with other NQTs within the school *and* in other establishments. Guidance and support with teaching in one's early days was appreciated, since this was a time when beginning teachers particularly need help with survival strategies. As they gained in experience and confidence, they looked for time and advice to enable them to engage in evaluation and reflection about their classroom practice.

The mentor was welcomed as someone who would offer NQTs approachability, support and confidentiality – a person with whom needs and worries could be aired candidly in order to avoid the feeling of being left on one's own. Another way of countering stress and worry in the induction year was for schools to take a sympathetic interest in NQTs' welfare – issues like their accommodation, transport arrangements or, that rare phenomenon in the first year of teaching, their social life!

The authors of the NFER report, Peter Earley and Kay Kinder, summed up their findings about effective induction as follows: it consisted of 'a planned but flexible programme of support that encompassed the development of skills, knowledge and expectations, and observation'. As such, they said, induction was not a cheap option in terms of the time and resources that need to be devoted to it. And as a result of their research, Earley and Kinder produced a conceptual framework identifying four models of induction support. Although they were not intended to be interpreted as different levels of effectiveness, nonetheless it was felt that the more sophisticated model has a greater chance of ensuring induction works well.

Reading 15.1

Mono-support systems

Responsibility for an NQT's induction was officially undertaken by a single person, usually in a senior management role. However, informal support might be sought from other personnel and official assessment functions undertaken by the head teacher or another senior staff member. This system more usually operated where a single NQT was appointed and was more common in primary schools.

Bi-support systems

The school offered support from a mentor (usually of middle management status such as a department head) in addition to a central induction programme involving the provision of information on school procedures and/or opportunities for discourse on teaching and learning issues. The latter was operated by senior management in the role of coordinator of induction.

Tri-support systems

[These] usually offered a combination of central meetings and/or supervision (involving senior staff), middle management mentor support (academic and/or pastoral) and, as well, another official designated personnel of near similar status, such as a 'buddy', a 'critical friend', a second i/c or year leader. This was being instituted as the overlap of assessment and support functions for official mentors sometimes proved problematic.

Multi-support systems

[These] offered support at a number of levels, but in addition had evidence of coordination between the levels. Thus, school induction managers running training and information sessions for mentors in their schools would be an example of a multi-support system. An example was where a head teacher attended the planning meetings of the NQT's year group and the mentor attended the school's central sessions along with the NQT. Joint training of mentors/NQTs featured in one LEA.

(Earley and Kinder 1994: 16–17)

It should go without saying that effective induction provision is an essential component of every NQT's first year in school. This was recognised in the James Report of 1971, although subsequent HMI surveys commented critically on the variable quality of induction. The most recent, in 1993, noted provision was better in secondary than primary schools, but pointed to the lack of smooth transition from ITT courses, through induction, to further professional development in the second year and beyond. Now, the DfEE has called for new teachers' individual needs to be set within a 'general programme of structured support, experience and further on-the-job training', with a particular focus on enabling NQTs to 'observe and learn from the best existing practice'.

The structural form that an effective induction process should take assumed increased significance in the years after statutory probation was abolished in 1992. The onus for its success has fallen squarely on schools, given the climate of devolved management in local authority and grant maintained schools, the delegation of INSET funds and the shrinkage of LEA inspector/adviser posts. Two surveys of Walsall schools, in 1993 and 1995, may well be typical of the wider situation in secondary schools.

Case study 15.1

Each school visited in the two surveys ran a central induction programme. There was a considerable degree of commonality in its key features. These include preparatory visits following appointment, obtaining information about the school and department, auditing the PGCE strengths and weaknesses of NQTs, arranging an INSET programme that included in-house 'twilight' sessions and off-site meetings, creating opportunities to undertake observations of experienced colleagues and visiting other schools. Subject-based training was generally regarded as a departmental responsibility.

Heads of department and senior managers (usually the person responsible for NQTs) observed lessons taught by NQTs. The format of this ranged from an informal chat after the lesson to a written, structured approach to observation with target setting for subsequent lessons.

Timetabled sessions were arranged in some schools for the NQTs to meet with a mentor to talk through any particular matters that arose. The atmosphere of support and interest that was shown to them by schools was regarded as being very important. A strong element of negotiation between the NQT and mentor was identified as a means of enabling provision to respond to each individual's needs, whether in the programme's initial planning or as issues presented themselves during the year.

The 'twilight' sessions covered a range of expected themes, such as styles of teaching and learning, classroom management and behaviour, display, assessment, pastoral issues, information technology, special needs, and even management issues like the role of the SMT and the school budget. One mentor spoke of starting with 'survival topics' and then moving the emphasis onto how the school works in order to 'guide NQTs onto their next professional level'. Issues covered during university courses were revisited. This was not seen as repetitive because they could now be applied to professional practice in the NQTs' new schools. Specialist staff were drafted in to lead particular sessions. The frequency of induction meetings varied – weekly, monthly or periodically – although all took place after school. Some concern was expressed about the diminishing nature of returns at such sessions after a full day's teaching.

NQTs expressed appreciation for the opportunity to spend time off-site, meeting other new teachers in order to share their concerns and reflections and achievements. A limited central programme run by the LEA provided one forum. There were also opportunities to visit other secondary schools to talk with, work alongside or observe subject specialists and to visit partner primary schools. However, the senior mentor in one GM school objected to having NQTs 'observing all over the place [since] you're only increasing the cost without increasing the come-back'! There was a worrying implication here, in that too introspective a focus restricts opportunities to share experiences with colleagues in other settings. It can breed an insular outlook.

All schools voiced concerns. A common complaint involved budget constraints, which meant NQTs were given timetable loads larger than the school wished. A similar issue was time for those mentoring the NQTs. Several schools expressed worries about the changed role of LEA inspectors and the loss of access for lesson observations.

(Abridged from Millar et al. 1993 and Bleach 1995)

During 1998, both the DfEE and TTA issued consultation documents identifying elements that should be included in every new teacher's induction year programme:

- opportunities to work with the best schools in the area, through visits to see good practice or by attendance at seminars and involving Advanced Skills Teachers (ASTs);
- mentoring by a member of staff designated as an 'induction tutor';
- observation of experienced teachers, again with a possible AST input;
- regular observation of teaching and feedback by mentors, ASTs, head teachers and LEA advisers;
- regular discussions with mentors to review professional practice, set targets and identify professional development activities;
- attendance on training courses to meet needs identified via the Career Entry Profiles and use of Induction Standards;
- visiting special schools and working with their school SENCO;
- contributing to school working parties and networking with NQTs in other schools.

So what is new? Little, it would seem, apart from proposals for creating opportunities to work with the 'best' schools and the 'best' teachers in the area or visit special schools. Schools that already provide well-targeted professional development and support for their NQTs will have few worries about this aspect of the new induction arrangements.

One important aspect of induction programmes concerns the value of beginning the process, not in September, but from the time of appointment. Many schools start to prepare their NQTs for the new school year by means of a day or two's induction in the latter part of the summer term, particularly once public examinations are over. It helps ease the beginning teacher over the transition shock that is all-too-common during the first days, or weeks, of the autumn term. Here is one structured approach recorded in the NFER survey:

Case study 15.2

This school had an induction policy stating that before appointment NQTs had certain entitlements, such as the opportunity to meet colleagues, obtain a timetable and receive an appropriate year group, department information, as well as details of the school and the LEA's programme of support. The programme consisted of:

Day 1: (with deputy) tour of school; introduction to key staff, office and support staff, office procedures explained; reprographics. Staffroom for coffee at break. Session in DH's room explaining: support systems for NQTs, feedback on previous NQTs' comments. Lunch in pub. Minibus tour for a view of catchment area, visit feeder primary schools, meet some Y6 pupils (future Y7). One hour session with Head of Upper and Lower School on pastoral provision. Documentation on school procedures/systems given in a pack the DH had developed.

Day 2: (in their departments) observing, schemes of work given plus lunch with department organised. Met again at end of day with DH to provide future access opportunities (telephone numbers over holidays, how to arrange future visits). Travelling expenses for these two days were paid by the school. Feedback from the NQTs was positive: the new teachers said they felt more part of the school and had already struck up positive relations with each other.

(Earley and Kinder 1994: 26)

A more philosophical approach to setting up induction would recognise the *principles* that should underpin it. This would acknowledge the NQT as an adult learner, begin from an analysis of his/her own practice, explicitly link learning and the workplace environment, promote shared reflection, focus on thoughts and feelings as well as actions, and integrate whole school and individual development. An essential challenge facing all induction managers and senior mentors is to translate these principles into action so that new professional colleagues experience an authentic culture of learning and reflection in which to embark upon their chosen careers.

Activity 15.2

A number of key themes emerged from the NFER's research into school induction programmes. Review your school's current provision in the light of this list. Are there any professional issues that you think you should add to what you already cover?

- pupil learning, e.g. able pupils, differentiation, special needs;
- teaching strategies, e.g. classroom management, discipline, flexible learning;

- administration of learning, e.g. parents' reports, record-keeping, target-setting;
- pastoral roles, e.g. PSME, form tutoring, child protection;
- school context, e.g. local community, governors, primary-secondary links;
- wider curriculum, e.g. vocational education, ICT, post-16 developments;
- NQT needs, e.g. time/stress management, career development;
- induction issues, e.g. use of CEP, observation procedures, feedback by NQTs.

Activity 15.3

Now think about what should be included on a pre-employment induction day:

- how would you prepare for the arrival of your NQT(s)?
- who are the most important people to introduce?
- what places in the school would you make a point of showing your NQT(s)?
- what key aspects of school organisation and procedure should be outlined?
- what essential documentation would you make available?
- what expectations and standards would you identify?

Identifying NQTs' individual needs

From September 1998, all NQTs taking up employment have had Career Entry Profiles (CEPs). As explained in Chapter 4, the Profile is a document summarising NQTs' particular strengths and priorities/weaknesses. It encourages schools to match development and training to identifiable individual needs, thereby creating a situation in which individualised action planning, monitoring and support can occur.

This is not a radically new departure. In 1987, the HMI survey, *The New Teacher in School*, noted that schools have problems in catering for new teachers as individuals. This was regarded as necessary given the variety of ages, experiences and backgrounds of people entering teaching. So it recommended that universities should provide schools with profiles detailing their strengths and weaknesses. Profiles subsequently formed part of the competence-based initiatives tried out in LEAs like Surrey, Clwyd and Walsall in the mid-1990s. Generally, they have proved to be successful in enabling induction to build on the knowledge, skills and competences acquired during ITT courses.

The TTA has explored another way of prompting schools to focus on each NQT's development needs by means of its feasibility study for an induction credit scheme. In 1997–98, it invited groups of schools to apply for a share of 200 induction credits, each worth £500. The scheme aimed to encourage schools to develop individualised programmes of NQT mentoring and support, taking into account priorities set out in their development plans, teaching standards and CEPs. One aim was to see how NQTs could be encouraged to take responsibility for their professional development after induction.

While the DfEE recognises that new teachers' individual development needs must be set within a general programme, the significance of schools' use of Career

Entry Profiles and the TTA's piloting of induction credits is clear: a blanket approach to induction will no longer do. In the future, there will be increasing pressures for support and induction to be targeted to individuals' needs. If this is recognised as good practice in the type of teaching and learning experiences offered to pupils, why shouldn't the principle of differentiation apply equally to how schools respond to the needs of new teachers?

This type of approach to induction and training makes sense as a recognition of the variation in background, age, experience and competence that NQTs bring to their first posts. One form of provision will not suit everyone. And as Chapter 5 explained, there are different stages that NQTs go through *during* their induction year. Broadly, issues of classroom survival and subject competence concern them at first. Then as the induction year progresses, their needs tend to be differentiated as they get to grips with curriculum and learning issues. NQTs often make their way through these stages at different rates of progress. While one new appointment in a school will demonstrate a learning curve that extends naturally upwards, another is just as likely to pursue a more erratic course.

Case study 15.3

I think my needs at the outset were essentially about surviving . . . and any help that I could receive was appreciated. In the spring term my needs have been more concerned with whether or not the strategies that I have employed are working and will they work with the new children, the reception children. Are the strategies that I've used for class organisation and for approaching the children any good; will they work again? So it's more a question of this and seeing how the children have responded to different techniques. (NQT: Primary)

(Earley and Kinder 1994: 91)

Identification of the individual's development needs has assumed significance for teachers well beyond the induction year. The effect of both appraisal and OFSTED inspections has been to stress the importance of assessing teachers' professional needs as a means of initiating change or improvement. Whatever the practical difficulties of implementing appraisal, it is widely regarded as a means of helping individuals improve their classroom performance by identifying needs and setting targets. Again, whatever OFSTED's flaws, the process entailed in framing the post-inspection action plan emphasises needs and targets for individuals, departments and schools. More recently, needs assessment has appeared as a formal process at the start of NPQH courses for aspirant head teachers.

In its basic form, individual needs assessment should involve mentors working with NQTs to:

- find out where they are at present in their professional competence;
- identify where they need to be in order to demonstrate progression;
- agree how they can be assisted in making that movement.

Once the need is defined and accepted, targets can be set for achieving the desired change or improvement, and support can be provided to try to ensure that they are met. If the process is genuinely concerned with individual development, one of the key functions of mentoring must be to ensure that the professional learning of the NQT does not become unduly subordinate to the needs of the department or the school.

So how should mentors go about identifying and assessing the individuals needs of their NQTs? What techniques can be employed to find the evidence that will inform and target training and development? And how can such needs assessment be undertaken in an atmosphere that avoids beginning teachers feeling threatened because of inevitable gaps in their knowledge, skills and competence? There are five key approaches:

- use of the Career Entry Profile for target-setting;
- observation of classroom practice;
- personal review meetings;
- reflective mentoring based on an active classroom teaching relationship;
- structured opportunities for critical self-reflection.

The starting point is the Career Entry Profile. Chapter 4 gives guidelines on practical ways of linking the CEP to QTS and Induction Standards, in terms of helping moving the new teacher forward. A meeting between the NQT and mentor to discuss the content of the Profile should be convened at the start of the school year. The document has three sections: Section A is a summary of the ITT course and Section B is a statement of strengths and priorities based on the course. Properly completed, the latter will provide a valuable source for exploring experiences and issues arising from ITT. Section C is the key developmental section, where NQT and mentor agree a way forward by target-setting and action planning, based on the needs assessment implicit in the content of the previous two sections. Targets should embody the SMART acronym (see Figure 15.2).

S – SPECIFIC

M – MANAGEABLE, MEASURABLE

A – APPROPRIATE, AGREED, ACHIEVABLE

R – REALISTIC, RELEVANT, RECORDED

T – TIME BONDED

Figure 15.2 SMART targets

Observation of classroom practice is the next step. It should comprise three essential stages: (a) a preliminary meeting to establish criteria for observation; (b) the observation itself, with a specific focus; (c) feedback in which NQT and mentor have the opportunity to discuss issues and use them, again, as the basis for defining needs. Of course, research has identified artificial factors associated with lesson observations – they tend to be restricted to one lesson, the notice given raises the possibility of 'special' lessons being delivered and the presence of the mentor can distort the reality of the pupils' behaviour and learning. So this aspect of needs assessment is not without difficulties.

Regular personal tutorial meetings with mentors will provide a further opportunity for reviewing an NQT's development. The agenda is likely to include his/her personal achievements, performance set against QTS and Induction Standards, and classroom observation and feedback. Appraisal interviews are already an established means of defining and agreeing targets. The use of simple logbooks, in which NQTs make self-reflective evaluations of their progress, would also inform discussion with the mentor.

One of the most powerful ways of gathering information for individual needs analysis is embodied in approaches to reflective mentoring. This involves the mentor acting as a reflective coach, as a critical friend or as a co-enquirer (see Table 15.1). All require an active pedagogical relationship between mentor and NQT. However, there are obvious implications for time and resources. A school's hierarchical organisation, the inflexibility of the timetable and the fact that most classrooms have four walls are other constraints!

Table 15.1 Reflective mentoring

Reflective coaching	NQT helped to think about and refine performance by an actively involved mentor who offers comments. Mentee's own professional experiences become basic material for learning about teaching, as mentor makes planned interventions to channel NQT's thinking.
Critical friend	Mentor challenges NQT to re-examine his/her teaching, while providing encouragement and support. Helps NQT shift focus from lessons as teaching opportunities for him/herself to how he/she can increase learning potential of pupils.
Co-enquirer	Priorities are negotiated, with NQT identifying focus for attention. Observation and collaborative teaching are key techniques, with NQT taking lead in analysing/evaluating performance and using mentor's record as basis for discussion. Diagnostic assessment and prescriptions for action tackled collaboratively by both.

(Adapted from Brooks and Sikes 1997: 23–8)

The other valid means of diagnosing NQTs' individual needs is to offer practical and structured opportunities for critical self-reflection in order to inform and improve their professional practice and thinking. The earlier chapters on reflective practice offer specific steps through such a strategy, whereby the NQT identifies an aspect of relevant interest or concern, reviews his/her existing practice and develops a possible solution, which is monitored and then evaluated in order to establish a 'claim' for improvement.

Activity 15.4

Reflect on how you, as a mentor, currently try to make an on-going needs assessment of your NQT(s). How far could any of the approaches suggested in this section be introduced at your school?

One important aspect of this work is maintaining a log of what takes place in your review meetings and of the training and development opportunities you provide. Design a simple form that would act as an induction record for NQTs in your school.

Chapter 16

Assessment, resources and quality assurance

Key issues

- *How can NQT self-assessment be encouraged and put into practice?*
- *What assessment benchmarks are there in the DfEE's induction arrangements?*
- *What ethical issues surround NQT assessment?*
- *What are the timing and resource implications for effective induction?*
- *How can schools assure the quality of induction and mentoring?*

NQT assessment

Certain guiding principles underpin the effective assessment of NQTs:

- Assessment is usually 'context-specific', so NQTs should be provided with a variety of opportunities and settings in which their competence may be assessed.
- Criteria for assessment should be shared and agreed in advance, so that both mentors and NQTs are conversant with them.
- Induction managers/senior mentors have a quality assurance role to ensure procedures for assessing NQTs are consistently applied in different parts of a school.
- NQTs should be assessed both formatively (e.g. lesson observation feedback and target-setting) and summatively (summing up progress on an interim termly basis and at the end of the induction year).
- All teachers who play a part in the NQT's development (e.g. other departmental staff, year heads and SENCO) should be involved in assessment in order to gain an all-round view of his/her performance.
- There should be opportunities for NQTs to exercise self-assessment, linked to the use of profiling and review meetings with their mentors.
- In view of a school's responsibility for assessing an NQT's competence to continue teaching beyond the induction year, procedures must be rigorous, but also fair, transparent and objective.

Self-assessment should form an integral part of each NQT's assessment programme during induction. Not being a process imposed from above, it has the advantage of reinforcing learning and development by encouraging a sense of 'ownership' about assessment. It enables NQTs to monitor their progress, analyse their performance and identify their training needs. It also feeds into activities designed to encourage reflective practice and the development of professional competence and understanding.

Despite all these advantageous outcomes, self-assessment cannot exist in isolation and is certainly not an easy task to master. NQTs entering schools have been provided with opportunities for critical self-analysis of their teaching on school attachments and have had the experience of completing Career Entry Profiles. However, careful support is still required if they are to engage successfully in self-assessment. At this early stage in their careers, their grasp of issues relating to teaching and learning will be restricted and they are likely to frame comments in the light of what they perceive to be their mentors' expectations. So self-assessment and evaluation needs to be complemented by regular review meetings with mentors and by the maintenance of some kind of log or profile.

To assist NQTs with the process, it could well be helpful to provide them with a self-assessment schedule, based on the Induction Standards. An example of what part of it could look like is given in Figure 16.1, using one of the Standards as a headline and then unpicking it into a number of indicators. The NQT would reflect on his/her performance against different aspects of the Standard and put a tick in the appropriate column. An additional space is provided for a comment. This could act as the basis for discussion with the mentor about strengths and weaknesses, along with other forms of evidence like lesson plans/evaluations and examples of pupils' work. Needless to say, it could be an exercise in unmanageable bureaucracy to try to get NQTs to unpick and review their progress against every Standard. So a more targeted approach lies in linking detailed discussion of selected Standards to individual NQTs' development needs, as identified in the CEP.

The DfEE's new induction arrangements are emphatic about the need to establish 'clear professional standards' for NQTs to meet when being assessed. They will not be able to complete the induction period satisfactorily unless they have demonstrated their mastery of the Qualified Teacher Status standards on an independent and sustained basis. Moreover, they must show that they have built on and progressed *beyond* the QTS standards. That is why the DfEE has drawn up a set of Induction Standards to act as a benchmark for the successful completion of induction from September 1999.

This continuing reliance on 'standards' reflects the prevailing utilitarian outlook in the DfEE and TTA regarding what constitutes an effective teacher. It sees teaching as an activity that can be broken down into small component parts, so that student and novice teachers can be 'trained' to perform those tasks and develop forms of behaviour in the most efficient way possible. Since the effective teacher is one who carries out *particular tasks* with expertise, teacher education

SELF-ASSESSMENT OF INDUCTION STANDARDS	1	2	3
Secures a good standard of pupil behaviour in the classroom			
Ensures beginnings and endings of lesson, and transition from one activity to another, are orderly			
Has clear, consistent ground rules and expectations which pupils understand, respect and follow			
Maintains watchful eye on pupils in all parts of classroom			
Acts to pre-empt inappropriate behaviour			
Deals with inappropriate behaviour in line with school policy			
Avoids confrontation			
Uses praise and encouragement to promote positive attitudes			
Key: 1 = Very good 2 = Satisfactory 3 = Needs improvement			
Comments			

Figure 16.1 Self-assessment of Induction Standards

and induction have to be centred on producing and verifying competence in those tasks. There is a strongly vocational nature to this philosophy that slots in comfortably with the Conservative New Right, and now New Labour, emphasis on 'training' rather than 'education'.

The competences and standards identified by the DfEE and TTA are essentially behaviourist and product-oriented in approach. They tend to reduce objectives to measurable outcomes and pre-specified ends – either you can do it or you can't! This reductionist view of the teacher's function, derived from a mechanistic analysis of work functions, could lead to a narrowing of one's professional role. However, there are other forms of competence that are concerned with a *broader aggregation of skills* and an ability to demonstrate higher level thinking and affective qualities, e.g.

- empathising with the concerns of others;
- making professional judgements;
- self-monitoring one's own conduct; or
- exercising authority in a manner consistent with professional ethics.

Surely what is required for induction and continuing professional development programmes is a model that encourages teachers to develop broad perspectives and to investigate and analyse practice.

Reading 16.1

Advocates of competence-based approaches claim that by specifying the outcomes which trainees must achieve, clear foci are provided for all those involved in the training process. This helps to ensure consistency of standards, providing a common training entitlement for all... Assessment is also made more rigorous. Competence-based frameworks reduce the subjectivity of the assessment, increasing employers' confidence in the credibility of the qualification... [NQTs] have a clearer idea of the goals at which they are aiming.

   Critics see competence-based assessment as a narrowing and mechanical approach which focuses attention on behaviour and skills. The capacity to perform certain skills and behaviours is no guarantee of an intelligent understanding of the underlying knowledge and concepts which inform professional practice. The demonstration of routine competences which can be ticked off on a checklist is of little value if it is not informed by real knowledge and insight into how, why and when certain skills work... True professionalism is the embodiment of certain qualities, values and attitudes which narrow competence-based models neglect. Thus critics object to the atomisation of professionalism, arguing that essential qualities are missed by such an approach. Not only is the professional person more than the sum of his or her parts, but it is also technically possible for an individual to satisfy the separate items on a list of competences while the total performance falls short of the standards expected of a professional person in that field.

(Brooks and Sikes 1997: 124)

Whatever one's concerns or reservations about this trend towards de-professionalisation, there can be no question of ignoring the DfEE and TTA's instrumental construction of teacher education and induction. A standards-based approach is an official requirement and all NQTs must demonstrate their competence, set against the prescribed standards, if they are to complete successfully their induction year.

Under the DfEE's new arrangements, the formal responsibility for monitoring and day-to-day assessment of the NQT rests with his/her immediate line manager. The induction tutor or mentor must hold progress discussions on a monthly basis, with a termly written record reviewing progress against the induction standards. At the end of the year, the school's head teacher is required to complete a formal written assessment based on:

- the induction tutor's reports;
- lesson observations;
- reports from any other teachers;
- evidence of achievement by the NQT's pupils;
- the Career Entry Profile and evidence from the NQT's self-assessments;
- any judgements made by OFSTED inspectors.

Local authorities have a role in moderating and ensuring the application of common quality standards across their schools. So the LEA is charged with validating the head's recommendation that an NQT has achieved the professional standards and should be confirmed as a member of the teaching profession.

Ethical issues

The DfEE's emphasis on line management and rigorous assessment contains possible tensions for mentors that researchers have already recognised. Put simply, mentors who have worked hard to build up close professional relationships with their NQTs may feel uncomfortable at the prospect of appearing unduly critical of somebody's competence or having to maintain a degree of 'distance' when making judgements. By the same token, new teachers may worry that their assessments could be affected if they constantly seek advice from their mentor. Another concern is that a poor assessment could be perceived as a reflection on the quality of a mentor's work with an NQT – the mentor may feel personally responsible for his/her difficulties. Consequently, mentoring practice in some schools has created a dichotomous situation whereby the counselling role is devolved to subject mentors, while senior staff gear themselves up for the more detached assessment role that LEA advisers previously held.

Under the DfEE's new procedures, the induction tutor carries the monitoring and assessment brief. Yet there need not necessarily be a conflict between this and the more affective and developmental aspects of their work. The way to reconcile the two roles of assessor and supporter, surely, is to enable one's NQTs to share in the ownership of the assessment process and to use the strength of the protégé–mentor relationship to guide them through whatever critical points need to be made. No one would deny it can be a knife-edge performance at times! And it is not likely to be successful if the mentor succumbs to the temptation to be reassuring rather than challenging, or offers comments that are subjective and judgemental.

Case study 16.1

I tend to be a direct person and will tell them what hat I've come in wearing. I think the clearer you make your intentions, the clearer they can see the division. It's not actually a division, because they feel involved in the assessment. They don't feel you are assessing them from on high, saying 'You haven't got this right'. (Senior mentor)

I could see a conflict arising if the assessment was done in a dogmatic way. But as it wasn't done like that, tension didn't arise. It's been done fairly. Along the way you've been told everything and you don't end up disagreeing with the assessor. (NQT)

It depends very much on what the mentor is like. She is an extremely friendly and helpful sort of person; not threatening at all. Her attitude has seemed to be 'I'm here to help' as opposed to 'I'm here to put down your bad points'. (NQT)

It's to do with personalities: the human face with which assessment is carried out. (NQT)

(Bleach 1995: 55)

An induction manager or mentor is likely to feel particular discomfort when the newly qualified teacher has serious problems or is at risk of failing. Problems encountered with failing NQTs include:

• ineffective classroom control
• an inability to establish themselves as a 'presence' with children
• inappropriate teaching and learning activities
• weak subject knowledge and understanding.

In the worst cases, there is a low *awareness* of the school/classroom context in which they are working and a low level of *capability* in terms of the knowledge, skills and experience they bring to teaching. John West-Burnham and Fergus O'Sullivan (1998) have characterised this lethal combination in terms of the 'classically incompetent' teacher, who is unaware of his/her personal performance and paucity of skills. In more redeemable cases, at least the awareness is high (the NQT understands what must be done to improve) or the capability is high (he/she has the necessary skills, but cannot yet make best use of them). The effective NQT, of course, knows what needs to be done *and* is able to deliver it!

Given the demanding nature of the QTS standards that student teachers now have to meet before being eligible for NQT status and taking up their first appointments, the vast majority of new teachers should not demonstrate low levels of awareness and capability. If difficulties *do* occur, the DfEE requires the NQT to be informed in writing that without specified improvement, his/her future is at risk. There are various strategies, of course, that induction managers and mentors can employ to help them:

• diagnose the precise nature of the problem (e.g. too informal a relationship with classes) and communicate an understanding of why the NQT is going wrong;
• set attainable targets for action, with specific and practical steps outlined for securing an improvement in practice;
• when progress is made, commend the NQT's achievement – as with children, it is often good for motivation to 'catch them being good';
• be upbeat and optimistic about the NQT's prospects for making a satisfactory improvement, so that he/she does not develop a mindset of failure;

- be honest and above-board about any continuing difficulties, while still giving support and advice – it may be necessary to be challenging or directive at times;
- use the technique of 'modelling', whereby the NQT can focus attention on particular aspects of teaching by observing a more experienced colleague exercising specific skills and strategies;
- maintain a documentary record of the difficulties encountered, how they are being addressed by the NQT and what support and counselling are being provided.

The DfEE's consultation paper on induction was explicit about what must be done in the event of an NQT irredeemably falling short in any of the professional standards: 'We believe that they should not be confirmed as members of the teaching profession.' To do anything else would be to put at risk pupils' education and the high standards of professional competence parents expect schools to display. One would not, after all, expect any less exacting a benchmark in one's solicitor or doctor or architect.

Where there is no useful purpose served in prolonging unsatisfactory performance, the recommendation at the end of induction should represent 'a clean and clear judgement' on why the NQT has failed to meet the statutory requirements and, therefore, should not be eligible to be employed further as a teacher. However, LEAs have the option of offering the individual the opportunity of up to a year's extension to the induction period in exceptional circumstances. There is a right of appeal by failed NQTs, initially to the Secretary of State and eventually to a General Teaching Council when it is formed. Although it is not mentioned by the DfEE, every school would be well advised to include an 'at risk' component in the assessment and quality assurance section of its induction policy. This will ensure that there is an explicit, effective and prompt mechanism in place so that no one is in any doubt about what needs to be done or what an NQT's entitlement is.

Activity 16.1

Problems that mentors encounter in NQTs include:

- too mild and soft-spoken a manner in front of pupils;
- a rigid and inflexible approach to pupils' behaviour;
- an unadventurous and unenthusiastic repertoire of teaching methods;
- a lack of personal organisation in the classroom;
- a failure to provide challenges for more able pupils;
- a reluctance to listen to advice and act upon it.

If you encountered one or more of these difficulties in an NQT, how would you, as a mentor, seek to raise his/her levels of awareness and capability?

Time, resources and quality assurance

The finite nature of time is a sensitive general issue for all teachers. Similarly, the provision of quality time for the guidance and assessment of NQTs is a crucial factor as far as induction managers and mentors are concerned. Various pieces of research show that while mentors express enjoyment about fulfilling their role and welcome the professional challenges it brings, time for mentoring is regarded as a commodity in insatiably short supply. In particular, more time is regarded as necessary for the developmental purposes of counselling NQTs and giving them feedback after lesson observations. NQTs themselves, of course, need time for subject and lesson planning.

Earley and Kinder's NFER survey in the early 1990s revealed that mentors often had serious difficulties in finding the time to sustain their developmental role with NQTs. Just as it was uncommon for classroom and subject mentors to be offered non-contact time specifically for induction work, so senior staff referred to the pressures of their various and extensive school-wide responsibilities.

Some mentors *are* fortunate enough to enjoy additional regular, protected non-contact time in which to have reflective discussions with their mentees, while most NQTs benefit from a modest reduction in their timetable and work loading in the first year. The DfEE's requirement from September 1999 is that the latter teach no more than 90 per cent of the average hours taught by main professional grade staff. For the majority of mentors, it is likely that the allocation of non-contact time is inadequate or non-existent, particularly in primary schools – with all the frustrations that causes.

Induction managers who are part of the senior staff team are expected to carry out the role as one of their (many) wider responsibilities, while heads of department find mentoring written into their role specification as part of the requirement to support and develop all their staff. Not surprisingly, therefore, surveys that dwell on the time issue report interviewees speaking of 'snatched time', 'the lack of quality time' or 'as and when'. Because some of the work done with NQTs is informal, it is not so easy to quantify. So mentors find themselves forced to use their own resourcefulness to create improvised opportunities at registrations, breaks, lunchtimes and out-of-school hours.

The intrinsic worth of the role, sometimes linked to benefits that are recognised in terms of one's professional development, is what keeps many mentors' commitment burning. Nevertheless, the 'crowded hours' into which their activities must be slotted creates conditions inimical to a high professional standard of mentoring. There is the fact, too, that the amount of time required will vary from NQT to NQT. Some work involves solving problems that are short-term or immediate in nature. Being 'rehabilitative', it follows a particular difficulty experienced by an individual, so would not slot into any formal mentoring time, even given adequate resources.

It is probably true to say that in most school budgetary decisions, provision for mentoring is not a priority, except to act as a conduit for whatever central funds are delegated by LEAs. Clarifying and costing the various roles and responsibilities of induction and mentoring does not occur. So one ends up with a situation in which the success of mentoring is due, in no small part, to the commitment mentors and NQTs make by using their own personal time. Clearly, this will not do. There is an onus upon head teachers to have a realistic understanding of the resource demands of the new induction arrangements. Induction and mentoring *should* be recognised as a legitimate call upon the 'quality' time of teachers and incorporated into development and budget planning as a basic requisite, rather than left to be dependent on individual teacher's goodwill. This should take practical expression in the form of earmarking resources for:

• regular lesson observations and reviews that are counted as contact time;
• timetabled meetings to facilitate reflection and discussion;
• buying in supply cover;
• funding administrative support, etc.

One must hope that the DfEE will be true to its word in stating that 'adequate targeted resources' will be available, via the Standards Fund, at all levels for its new induction arrangements. And head teachers must remember that they are now accountable to LEAs and OFSTED for the appropriate use of these resources at school level.

Activity 16.2

It is important for a school's management to have a realistic understanding of the commitment required by induction and mentoring in terms of time and resources expended over a year. Think about the induction scheme you have run, or have been involved with, this year. Itemise the different aspects of it (e.g. lesson observations, staff time for mentoring meetings, INSET courses) and try to work out an approximate costing.

LEAs and OFSTED have key parts to play in assuring the quality of the DfEE's new induction arrangements. Since the local authorities have an overall responsibility for the quality of induction in their role as 'appropriate bodies', they are now supposed to:

• ensure that head teachers and governors are aware of their responsibilities;
• consult with them on the nature and extent of quality assurance procedures;
• ensure that induction review forms an integral part of scheduled visits to schools by their link inspectors;
• advise schools on good practice;
• be ready to provide additional advice and guidance for NQTs who are not making satisfactory progress;
• ensure that there is consistent practice and deal with any appeals.

OFSTED inspection teams will henceforth include induction in their scrutiny of schools, armed with their usual brief to ascertain its impact on the quality of teaching and learning in the classroom and whether it offers value for the resources invested. A future quality assurance role also awaits the General Teaching Council when it is formed. This use of external agencies is all very well, but individual head teachers and induction managers themselves have a clear responsibility for developing procedures that evaluate the design, delivery and outcomes of their induction programmes. These will need to take account of national induction requirements and the organisational cultures of their own institutions.

Several quality assurance questions arise from the work of subject/classroom mentors in ensuring that high standards are consistently and objectively applied. Induction managers/senior mentors have a crucial part to play in seeking answers, based on discussions with the mentor themselves, feedback from NQTs and their general awareness of practice in the school, e.g.

- what criteria are used to select mentors and do these result in effective mentors?
- have they received effective training?
- are they carrying out their duties successfully?
- are mentors in a large school providing for NQTs in a consistent manner?
- how can one be sure they are exercising consistency in their judgement of NQTs?
- are mentors being given support and feedback?
- if the quality is not good enough, what action is then taken?

Similarly, in the assessment of NQTs there must be effective procedures and criteria. Appropriate points to scrutinise include:

- how does the school define what is expected of effective assessment procedures?
- how is assessment evidence obtained and how is its reliability checked?
- how does the school ensure consistency of judgement between departments?
- are assessment procedures transparent to all participants?
- how is it decided whether the quality of assessment procedures is good enough?
- what action is then taken and how are the results monitored?

Reading 16.2 illustrates some ways that schools have tried to monitor the quality of mentoring in initial teacher education partnerships.

Reading 16.2

Ensure mentoring is given a high profile within the school

Students have an entitlement to a well structured and supportive school experience. Mentors have an entitlement to the time and training that will enable them to be effective in their work...This will not happen if mentors are expected to debrief students during their morning break or have their allocated mentoring time 'cut' to teach absent colleagues' classes.

Establish mechanisms for student feedback

The views of students should be built into the regular evaluation of the programme...through both informal discussions and more formal questionnaires.

Include mentoring within staff appraisal

As an important part of the teacher's professional role, mentoring should be built into the school's regular appraisal procedures.

Encourage self-evaluation

Mentors should be encouraged to keep a record of their work with students. They should be encouraged to reflect critically on both the quality of their mentoring and on the model of good practice that they present to students.

Encourage mutual learning support

Mentors are likely to benefit from sharing their experiences with others both inside and outside the school. This is particularly important in small schools.

(Maynard 1997: 17)

One of the points in Reading 16.2 mentions the usefulness of questionnaires for gaining feedback in order to keep quality under continuous review. The next extract is a good example of an attempt to monitor the learning that has taken place during the mentoring relationship.

Reading 16.3

Questionnaire for mentors

- What do you think has been your major contribution to the NQT's development?
- What would you do differently next time?
- How do you think you have developed during this year's mentoring experience?
- What aspects of mentoring have you particularly enjoyed? What have you not enjoyed, or feel that you would benefit from further support with?
- In what ways has the school supported you in your role? What, within the organisation of the school, has been unhelpful or made life difficult?
- What changes, if any, would you suggest for the induction programme for NQTs?

Questionnaire for newly qualified teachers

- What have you gained from your support from your mentor?
- What have you enjoyed? What, if anything, have you found difficult or unhelpful?
- What single thing has been the most positive aspect? What single thing has been the most negative aspect?
- What – within the organisation of the school – has helped or hindered your experience of mentoring support?
- What would you suggest to improve mentoring support?
- What changes would you suggest to the overall induction programme for NQTs?
- What advice would you give to new teachers beginning a mentoring partnership?

(Abridged from Beels and Powell 1994: 42–3, 51)

Bibliography

Acton, R., Kirkham, G. and Smith, P. (1992) *Mentoring: A Core Skills Pack*. Alsager: Crewe and Alsager College of Higher Education.

Adler, S. (1991) 'The reflective practitioner and the curriculum of teacher education', *Journal of Education for Teaching* **17** (2), 139–50.

Adler, S. and Goodman, J. (1986) 'Critical theory as a foundation for methods courses'. *Journal of Teacher Education* **37** (4), 2–8.

Ashcroft, K. and Griffiths, M. (1989) 'Reflective teachers and reflective tutors: school experience in an initial teacher education course', *Journal of Education for Teaching* **15** (1), 35–52.

Association for Science Education *Systematic Classroom Observation*. London: ASE.

Barnfield, J., Bleach, K., Lowe, D. and Rochfort, S. (1994) *Managing Quality Induction: A Competency Based Approach*. Walsall: Walsall LEA Inspectorate.

Beels, C. and Powell, D. (1994) *Mentoring with Newly Qualified Teachers – The Practical Guide*. Leeds: CCDU University of Leeds.

Bleach, K. (1995) *Making The Most of Mentoring: A Study of the Dynamics of the Mentoring Relationship with NQTs in Five Walsall Schools*. Unpublished MA dissertation: Warwick University.

Bleach, K. (1997) 'The importance of critical self-reflection in mentoring newly-qualified teachers', *Mentoring and Tutoring* **4** (3), 19–24.

Bleach, K. (1998) 'Self-reflection: an aid to NQTs' practice', *Professional Development Today* **1** (3), 7–15.

Booth, M. (1993) 'The effectiveness and role of the mentor in school: the students' view', *Cambridge Journal of Education* **23** (2), 185–97.

Boydell, D. (1994) 'Relationships and feelings: the affective dimension to mentoring in the primary school', *Mentoring and Tutoring* **2** (2), 37–44.

Bridges, D. and Kerry, T. (eds) (1993) *Developing Teachers Professionally*. London: Routledge.

Brooks, V. and Sikes, P. (1997) *The Good Mentor Guide*. Buckingham: Open University Press.

Burton, L. and Povey, H. (1996) 'Competency in the mathematics classroom – the example of equal opportunities', in Hustler, D. and McIntyre, D. (eds) *Developing Competent Teachers*, 128–40. London: David Fulton Publishers.

Capel, S., Leask, M. and Turner, T. (1997) *Starting to Teach in the Secondary School*. London: Routledge.

Carr, W. (1995) *For Education: Towards Critical Educational Inquiry*. Buckingham: Open University Press.

Corbett, P. and Wright, D. (1994) 'Issues in the selection and training of mentors for school-based primary initial teacher training', in McIntyre, D. *et al.* (eds) *Mentoring: Perspectives on School-Based Teacher Education*, 220–33. London: Kogan Page.

Cruikshank, D. (1987) *Reflective Teaching*. Virginia: Association of Teacher Educators.

Dann, R. (1996) 'Teacher-mentor to teacher-researcher', *Mentoring and Tutoring* **3** (3), 33–7.

DES (1985) *Better Schools*. London: HMSO.

Devlin, L. (1995) 'The mentor' in Glover, D. and Mardle, G. (eds) *The Management of Mentoring*, 64–84. London: Kogan Page.

Dewey, J. (1933) 'Why reflective thinking must be an educational aim', in Archambault, R. (ed.) (1964) *John Dewey on Education: Selected Writings*. Chicago: University of Chicago Press.

DFE (1992) *Initial Teacher Training (Secondary Phase)*. Circular 9/92. London: DFE.

DfEE (1998) *Induction for New Teachers. A Consultation Document*. London: DfEE.

DfEE (1999) *The Induction Period for Newly Qualified Teachers*. Circular 5/99. London: DfEE.

Earley, P. and Kinder, K. (1994) *Initiation Rights: Effective Induction Practices for New Teachers*. Slough: NFER.

Elliott, B. and Calderhead, J. (1994) 'Mentoring for Teacher Development: Possibilities and Caveats', in McIntyre, D. *et al.* (eds) *Mentoring: Perspectives on School-Based Teacher Education*, 166–89. London: Kogan Page.

Elliott, J. (1988) Teachers as researchers: implications for supervision and teacher education. Paper presented at the Annual Meeting of the American Educational Research Association: New Orleans.

Elliott, J. (1989) 'Educational theory and the professional learning of teachers: an overview', *Cambridge Journal of Education* **19** (1), 81–101.

Fidler, B. and Lock, N (1994) *Mentorship and Whole-school Development*. London: Longman/BEMAS.

Freire, P. (1970) *Pedagogy of the Oppressed*. New York: Seabury Press.

Frost, D. (1994) 'Reflective mentoring and the new partnership', in McIntyre, D. *et al.* (eds) *Mentoring: Perspectives on School-Based Teacher Education*, 130–45. London: Kogan Page.

Furlong, J., Maynard, T., Miles, S. and Wilkin, M. (1994) *The Secondary Active Mentoring Programme 1: Principles and Processes*. Cambridge: Pearson.

Glover, D. and Gough, G. (1995) 'Interaction and impact', in Glover, D. and Mardle, G. (eds) *The Management of Mentoring*, 135–46. London: Kogan Page.

Glover, D., Gough, G and Johnson, M. (1994) 'Towards a taxonomy of mentoring', *Mentoring and Tutoring* **2** (2), 25–30.

Glover, D. and Mardle, G. (eds) (1995) *The Management of Mentoring*. London: Kogan Page.

Hagger, H., Burn, K. and McIntyre, D. (1993) *The School Mentor Handbook*. London: Kogan Page.

Hagger, H. and McIntyre, D. (1994) *Mentoring in Secondary Schools. Reading 8: Learning Through Analysing Practice*. Milton Keynes: Open University.

Haykin, W., Pierce, A. and Stewart, I. *A Strategy for Appraisal*. Leeds: CCDU University of Leeds.

Healey, C. and Welchert, A. (1990) 'Mentoring relations: a definition to advance research and practice', *Educational Researcher* **19**, 17–21.

Heilbronn, R. and Jones, C. (eds) (1997) *New Teachers in an Urban Comprehensive School*. Stoke: Trentham Books.

HMI (1982) *The New Teacher in School 1982*. London: HMSO.

HMI (1988) *The New Teacher in School 1987*. London: HMSO.

Hunt, J. (1992) *Managing People at Work*. London: McGraw-Hill.

Hustler, D. and McIntyre, D. (eds) (1996) *Developing Competent Teachers*. London: David Fulton Publishers.

Hyland, T. (1993) 'Training, competence and expertise in teacher education', *Teacher Development* **2** (2), 117–122.

Imison, T. (1997) 'Hampstead School as a learning community', in Heilbronn, R. and Jones, C. *New Teachers in an Urban Comprehensive School*, 9–20. Stoke: Trentham Books.

James Committee (1972) *Teacher Education and Training*. London: HMSO.

Johnson, G. and Scholes, K. (1993) *Exploring Corporate Strategy*. London: Prentice Hall International.

Johnson, M. (1995) 'The professional mentor', in Glover, D. and Mardle, G. (eds) *The Management of Mentoring*, 85–97. London: Kogan Page.

Kolb, D. and Fry, R. (1975) 'Toward an applied theory of experiential learning', in Cooper, C. (ed.) *Theories of Group Processes*. London: Wiley.

Liston, D. and Zeichner, K. (1990) 'Reflective teaching and action research in pre-service teacher education', *Journal of Education for Teaching* **16** (3), 235–54.

Maynard, T. (ed.) (1997) *An Introduction to Primary Mentoring*. London: Cassell.

Maynard, T. and Furlong, J. (1993) 'Learning to teach and models of mentoring', in McIntyre, D. *et al.* (eds) *Mentoring: Perspectives on School-Based Teacher Education*, 69–85. London: Kogan Page.

McCulloch. M. and Fidler, B. (eds) (1994) *Improving Initial Teacher Training?* Harlow: Longman.

McIntyre, D. and Hagger, H. (1994) 'Teachers' expertise and models of mentoring', in McIntyre, D. *et al.* (eds) *Mentoring: Perspectives on School-Based Teacher Education*, 86–102. London: Kogan Page.

McIntyre, D. and Hagger, H. (eds) (1996) *Mentors in Schools*. London: David Fulton Publishers.

McIntyre, D., Hagger, H. and Wilkin, M. (eds) (1994) *Mentoring: Perspectives on School-Based Teacher Education.* London: Kogan Page.

Millar, B., Moran, M. and Lowe, D. (1993) *Induction of NQTs across Walsall Secondary Schools.* Report to Walsall LEA Inspectorate.

OFSTED (1993) *The New Teacher in School 1992.* London: HMSO.

Schön, D. (1983) *The Reflective Practitioner.* New York: Basic Books.

Schön, D. (1987) *Educating the Reflective Practitioner.* San Francisco: Jossey-Bass.

Sikes, P. and Troyna, B. (1991) 'True Stories: a case study in the use of life history in initial teacher education', *Educational Review* **43** (1), 3–16.

Smith, P. and West-Burnham, J. (1993) *Mentoring in the Effective School.* London: Longman.

Smith, R. and Alred, G. (1994) 'The impersonation of wisdom' in McIntyre, D. *et al.* (eds) *Mentoring: Perspectives on School-Based Teacher Education*, 103–16. London: Kogan Page.

Smyth, J. (1989) 'Developing and sustaining critical reflection in teacher education', *Journal of Teacher Education* **38** (4), 25–31.

Stronach, I., Cope, P., Inglis, B. and McNally, J. (1996) 'Competence guidelines in Scotland for initial teacher training: supercontrol or superperformance?' in Hustler, D. and McIntyre, D. (eds) *Developing Competent Teachers*, 72–85. London: David Fulton Publishers.

Tickle, L. (1989) 'On probation: preparation for professionalism', *Cambridge Journal of Education* **19** (3), 277–85.

Tickle, L. (1993) 'The first year of teaching as a learning experience', in Bridges, D. and Kerry, T. (eds) *Developing Teachers Professionally*, 79–92. London: Routledge.

TTA (1998) *Induction for Newly Qualified Teachers. Recommendations on Monitoring, Support and Assessment Arrangements. A Consultation Document.* London: TTA.

TTA (1999) *Career Entry Profile for Newly Qualified Teachers.* London: TTA.

Turner, M. (1993) 'The complementary roles of the head teacher, the mentor and the advisory teacher in induction and school-based teacher training', *Mentoring* **1** (2), 30–6.

Vonk, J. (1993) 'Mentoring beginning teachers: mentor knowledge and skills', *Mentoring* **1** (1), 31–41.

Webb, E. (1996) 'Missing the mark of quality', *Times Educational Supplement* 28/6/96, 4.

West-Burnham, J. and O'Sullivan, F. (1998) *Leadership and Professional Development in Schools.* London: *Financial Times*/Pitman Publishing.

Wilkin, M. (ed.) (1992) *Mentoring in Schools.* London: Kogan Page.

Williams A (1993) 'Teacher perceptions of their needs as mentors in the context of developing school-based initial teacher education', *British Educational Research Journal* **19** (4), 407–20.

Zeichner, K. and Liston, D. (1987) 'Teaching student teachers to reflect', *Harvard Educational Review* **57** (1), 23–48.

Index